JOURNEYS OF HEARTACHE AND GRACE

Conversations and Life Lessons from
Young People With Serious Illnesses
by Melody Chatelle

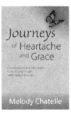

Pre-publication
Comments from Readers

"What we learn from a child's journey of sickness should be a road map of how we ought to live our lives each day. From reading *Journeys of Heartache and Grace*, you cannot miss making your life better as you progress on your own journey."

Karen R. Johnson
CEO, United Ways of Texas
Austin, Texas

"It's seldom that one reads a book that truly paints a three-dimensional picture of the fragile lives of others. Not only does Melody create a visualization through her interviews that is etched in the mind of the reader, it has you living and breathing the lives and losses of their families. This is a must read for families of children with severe illnesses and caregivers alike."

Bill M. Wooten, Ph.D.
Academic Medical Center
Houston, Texas

"As I read *Journeys of Heartache and Grace*, stories based on Melody Chatelle's interviews with sick or dying kids, I could not help but picture her kind, accepting face as she spoke with them. Melody's own generous qualities helped her elicit frank and powerful true stories about what her subjects experienced and how they would like to be treated in the face of life-threatening illness. Her conversations with their parents are equally compassionate and revealing.

This book is a must read for anyone who wants to support a loved one through a time of illness and probable death. Melody Chatelle has drawn wise guidance from the mouths of children and her book provides straightforward answers to the difficult question: How can I help?"

Joy H. Selak, Ph.D., Author
You Don't LOOK Sick! Living
Well with Invisible Chronic Illness
Austin, Texas

Prepublication Comments from Readers

"This book is a testament to those young individuals who are facing their own sickness and mortality—and the undeniable spirit for living each day to its fullest that they all share. We can all learn something from this book and the lessons these children share in a very open, honest and inspiring way."

Kim Carlos
Co-Author of *Nordie's at Noon*
Kansas City, Missouri

❦

"Years ago I had the privilege of taking a class from Elizabeth Kubler Ross, whose work on grief continues to help pave the way for experiencing tough times in smart ways. *Journeys of Heartache and Grace* does just the same by letting us know up front what young people are thinking about during situations we all face, either firsthand or with our loved ones. If you've ever wondered what to say when someone is really sick, this book is a must read."

The Honorable Ron Kirk
Former Texas Secretary of State and Mayor of Dallas
Dallas, Texas

"Much of my professional career has been spent writing and lecturing on leadership development. Yet from personal experience, I know that going through times of serious illnesses with our loved ones or ourselves is challenging and difficult, even for the strongest of leaders. Much of the time we feel at a loss for words, especially words of comfort and help, to share with others whom we care about. *Journeys of Heartache and Grace* will go a long way in helping us to meet that challenge."

The Honorable Sarah Weddington
Author, Attorney,
Former Presidential Advisor and Texas Legislator
Austin, Texas

❦

"I have been profoundly inspired by the courage, strength and optimism of children facing serious or terminal illnesses. Just as I have learned from them to embrace life everyday, everyone reading this book will be deeply touched and moved to fully embrace the blessings of life."

The Honorable Chet Edwards
Member, United States Congress
Washington, D.C.

Pre-publication Comments from Readers

"Melody Chatelle takes us on a non-academic, heartfelt journey into the minds and hearts, words and actions, and reactions and responses of several youngsters prematurely living their last seasons of life. Each one—like all of us—reflects distinct, individual characteristics and each one invites us to wonder how will we live into our last season and how would we do so as companions to another. Take the journey of heartache and grace. Let your heart ache; and through the words of others, imagine yourself in the journey."

The Reverend Carl Rohlfs
Senior Pastor
University United Methodist Church
Austin, Texas

"I had never asked the question about a dissertation being a 'life's work' before. The inquiry was so pointed that I worried that I would get a politically correct rather than a candid answer. But without hesitation, Melody answered, 'This is the work of my life.' From that moment on, that was my criterion for being a guide and helper: Keep Melody focused on the work of her life. The steps Melody took to write this book are evidence of the truth of that statement."

Larry Browning, Ph.D.
Professor
The University of Texas at Austin
Austin, Texas

"Through stories that bring out the paradox of our humanity—joy and suffering mysteriously intertwined—these children and their families communicate to us in no uncertain terms that love and suffering are the fabric of our human existence and are necessarily of great interest to health care professionals involved in caring for the sick. In the richness of their human experiences, we can discover that suffering and death can be transcended when experienced in the context of meaningful, healing relationships."

Javier R. Kane, M.D.
Director, Palliative and End-of-Life Care
St. Jude Children's Research Hospital
Memphis, Tennessee

To my dear
long-distance
friend and colleague,
Kippy –

Journeys
of Heartache
and Grace

Thanks
for in<u>spir</u>ing me,
<u>teaching</u> me, <u>amazing</u> me
me and <u>help</u>ing me
and <u>so many</u> –
Here's to life!

Melody

2010

Journeys
of Heartache
and Grace

Conversations and Life Lessons
From Young People
With Serious Illnesses

Melody Chatelle

LANGMARC
PUBLISHING
Austin, Texas

Journeys of Heartache and Grace

Conversations and Life Lessons From Young People With Serious Illnesses

By Melody Chatelle

Cover Design: Michael Qualben
Cover Photograph: Lifetouch Church Directories and Portraits

Copyright © 2008 by Melody Chatelle
First Printing: 2008
Printed in the United States of America

PUBLISHED BY
LangMarc Publishing
P.O. 90488
Austin, Texas 78709-0488
www.langmarc.com

Library of Congress Control Number: 2008905864
ISBN: 1880-292-351

DEDICATION

To family and friends for making dreams come true
to Edward R. Zamora
and in honor of my nieces,
Lauren and Rachel Wortham

to Dr. Javier Kane and Dr. Martha Morse
for opening research doors;

to the outstanding professors and staff at
The University of Texas at Austin
College of Communication Studies;

to the person, personification and perseverance of
Irma Jeanne Chatelle;

and ultimately

to all those who took the time to tell their stories of
hope, healing, heartache and grace.

TABLE OF CONTENTS

FOREWORD

Once every week I sit around a conference table with my staff to review the plans of care for our patients. Each patient has been certified as terminally ill by a physician. Our nurses and medical director intently scrutinize medication lists and evaluate patient compliance. They review vital signs, assess nutrition and hydration issues and monitor disease progression. Social workers report on family dynamics that help and hinder effective care and attend to end-of-life concerns like advance directives and do-not-resuscitate orders. Health care aides report on the patient's mobility and ability to perform daily living activities. And because dying is a markedly spiritual process, chaplains keep us posted on the existential issues that characterize the patient's journey to the end of life.

As we "team" each patient and steward a process that we truly believe gives us an honest assessment of the patient's condition, more often than not it's a story that gives us the real insight needed to insure that care is personalized and compassionate. Often a team member shares a story about a patient's response to treatment or some family dynamic that helps us truly understand the needs of the patient. I've learned that in dying, as in living, it takes a story to really understand another's circumstances.

The medical community has made remarkable strides in treating illness primarily because today's patient care rides the technological wave that characterizes modern medicine. Diagnosis is faster and prognosis more accurate because the physician's bag has been replaced with the physician's computer. Access to medical data and technology is revolutionizing health care faster than in previous generations. No one doubts the importance of technology in the practice of medicine.

Yet our expanding confidence in technology tempers the reality of the human experience. The truth is: not even the best of technologies can ultimately keep death at bay. Eventually each of our lives intersects the life of someone – a loved one, a colleague, a mentor, a neighbor who must steer the course to life's end. Every intersection is also cause to ponder our own mortality. In chronic and terminal illness, technology is powerless to bring meaning and hope. In the face of death, technology must yield to relationship, both human and divine, and the loving willingness of human beings to journey with those who contend with life-limiting illness.

While many of us are authentically willing to take the journey, as a society we're poorly equipped to travel the road. The reasons are myriad. Fear, misplaced trust in technological advances, denial all play a part. Melody Chatelle's *Journeys of Heartache and Grace* is a welcome place to begin the process of becoming better equipped, to garner guidance and counsel, in our efforts to engage and care for those who are seriously ill. Her stories of children are poignant and powerful, giving emotional insight that is unabashedly honest and unhampered by adult techniques that conceal true thoughts and feelings. The stories reveal fears and joys in honest ways that only children can express. Each story is a jewel that glistens with insight and sheds light on how to help us hear honestly and communicate courageously about topics that are uncomfortable and unpleasant.

This is not a book that articulates a philosophy about life and death. It is in many ways a how-to manual that challenges us to enter deeply into the lives of children and learn techniques that are the handiwork of authentic love and service. This book is sometimes difficult; yet it is always meaningful.

Michael Kearney, an Irish palliative physician, has written this about the pain of terminal illness: "It is proposed that while there is an abusive and useless dimension to illness, pain and suffering which needs to be removed if at all possible, there is also potential in such experience (no matter how unpleasant the experience is)....it is as though a dragon (that is the patient's distress) also guards a treasure – something essential for that particular individual's healing at that moment of time."

Journeys of Heartache and Grace is a marvelous step in slaying the dragon. It provides something essential for the healing of both the patient and the reader.

Craig Borchardt, Ph.D.
President and CEO
Hospice Brazos Valley, Inc.
Bryan, Texas

Help us to live as those who are prepared to die.
Methodist Church bulletin

PREFACE

Journeys of Heartache and Grace is a positive, practical book about end-of-life communication. It is a compilation of rich, funny, and tough stories that will touch you and leave a lasting impression. It's a grand narrative told in individual pieces straight from young people who are staring death in the face. Some of these young people are winning the fight; most are not.

The purpose of the book is to peer through a one-way window at an inevitable time when we or those we love are dying. *Journeys of Heartache and Grace* is about life and living and what to do and say during a time in which most of us are clueless or speechless. It offers practical communication insights (or suggestions) on how to interact with someone who is dying. The reader shares in the message delivered from those who are dying or facing grave illnesses.

The power and value of stories first came to me more than twenty years ago when I was given a small, beautifully written book by Anne Morrow Lindbergh entitled *Gift from the Sea*. The book is a profound and poignant look at life's simplification and serenity. I loved rereading the book at different times in my life when things seemed to be spinning out of control. As I've grown older, what has moved me is the reality that Ms. Lindbergh wrote *Gift from the Sea*, a book of hope and inspiration, after the tragic kidnapping and death of her son in the 1930s. Such a tragedy could have immobilized Ms. Lindbergh; yet it did not.

Journeys of Heartache and Grace is a book of hope and inspiration, too, as told by young people who are experiencing end-of-life times, yet who are still moving forward. I share my own story where I describe the deaths of my mother and grandmother within a 12-day period and what I learned from that grueling, painful experience. Following that traumatic event came a series of interviews with 13 seriously ill young people, their parents, hospice professionals, physicians, clergy, and others. These heartfelt interviews eventually culminated into my doctoral dissertation upon which *Journeys of Heartache and Grace* is based. This book presents life lessons for all through the eyes and words of children and young people.

The fact that more than half of the young people interviewed for *Journeys of Heartache and Grace* have since died is disheartening and sad for me, given the privilege I had of meeting them personally. Most of the young people interviewed wanted to tell their stories. Since these patients were willing to share their thoughts and feelings and in their own way teach in the midst of chemotherapy treatments, hospital stays, and times of remission, we will do well to listen and learn from their cherished messages.

Through this book's practical suggestions, we can better understand what spoken words are helpful to those who are dying as we interact with them. More importantly, we can learn what *not* to say to suffering people.

Each of the stories is different. We can laugh, cry, ponder, and pontificate what each story means to us personally. Pediatric providers working in hospice care can expand their professional horizons from reading words spoken by young people who are critically ill or dying and, in the process, offering us sage advice for serving others in similar situations. Clergy who sometimes feel overwhelmed in working with dying individuals can find new ways of responding.

Those who are wrestling with chronic disease in their own lives every single day can gain inspiration from others, including those patients who may be much younger. Parents of seriously ill young people can use *Journeys of Heartache and Grace* as a springboard for action and response and hope for the immediate future. Friends and neighbors are reminded not to stay away from the terminally ill but to show up, listen, and give hope.

This book is for everyone since we all will face end-of-life times. It's one of the few certain story endings we all share. Let us learn together.

Melody Chatelle

From a Physician's Perspective

Javier R. Kane, M.D.

Few things in life are more heartrending than witnessing the devastation a serious illness can cause in the lives of young and vulnerable patients. That painful reality is evident throughout this book. Serious illness can shatter all aspects of a child's life and can precipitate physical, emotional, and spiritual distress for the child and the family. Cancer and its therapy can ravage a child's body like no other illnesses and treatments. Children with cancer experience severe pain and multiple distressing symptoms that interfere with the activities of daily living, such as walking, eating, playing, and sleeping. Many of these symptoms also interfere with the child's ability to remain in school or live a normal life. The threat of pain from medical procedures and discomfort from adverse side effects of cancer treatments, as well as the fear of possible progression of the illness, are ever present for these patients and their families.

Emotional distress may be prominent for these children, particularly at the end of life, when they can experience anxiety, sadness or depression, and diminished pleasure. Many children also experience irritability, nervousness, and excessive worry. They may mourn the loss of their ability to function normally, and many carry their burdens in silence in an effort to avoid upsetting their loved ones. Moreover, children may struggle with adult-size existential questions about life and the meaning of illness without having a repertoire of personal experiences adequate to enable them to resolve these issues on their own.

Serious chronic illness also has a devastating effect on families. An unpredictable illness can bring about extended times of pronounced stress, which may lead a family to encounter problems adjusting effectively to the threats of serious illness and other life challenges. Indeed, illness is experienced by children as unique individuals but also as members of a functional family unit. Upon diagnosis of a serious illness, the families are often thrown into the medical establishment, where parents feel the need to surrender control of their child's well-being to the medical team.

Parents of seriously ill children may experience strong grief reactions, and many suffer from overwhelming fatigue or struggle attending to their own jobs. These parents may also struggle with feelings of fear, hopelessness, isolation, and an overall sense of inadequacy in protecting their children, and many grieve the loss of the future that they had imagined for their child. Siblings of a seriously ill child may feel abandoned by their parents and often are uninformed, confused about the changing structure of their environment, and worried about their sibling's condition and the well-being of their family. Finally, parents and siblings of the sick child may experience anticipatory grief as they await a child's imminent death.

Given the tremendous amount of physical, emotional, and spiritual suffering that seriously ill children and their families experience, it is amazing to see how resilient these children are and how families work to adjust emotionally and socially in even the most difficult of circumstances. Many healing relationships are established within the health care system and resources at a variety of levels are available to promote adequate coping skills for these families. The emotional, social and spiritual support provided by doctors, nurses, psychologists, social workers, child life and spiritual care personnel, and other staff members are essential to the healing process, as well as having access to relevant information about the illness and its treatment. An important point is to ensure comfort and relief from distressing symptoms. The presence of physical distress from symptoms may exacerbate emotional and even spiritual distress.

Additionally, creating an open and safe environment where children and family members can express their concerns about the illness and its treatment, as well as fears about death and what the future might bring, is also an important task for caregivers. Fostering social support and helping the child or adolescent to continue to be engaged in task-oriented activities and typical activities of daily living (i.e., school, play, and social engagements) is also important. Ensuring access to supportive care services (i.e., social work, spiritual care, and child life) and treatment utilizing behavioral techniques (i.e., distraction, relaxation, training, and imagery) may be useful in reducing anxiety and even certain physical symptoms. Finally, facilitating access to helpful information is of utmost importance to ensure that the child, when indicated, and his or her family feel empowered to effectively participate in the process of making decisions about their care.

Serious illness involves a dynamic process of evolving intrapersonal, interpersonal, and transpersonal relationships and communications. Throughout this process, in which health care providers dedicate themselves to caring for the sick, establishing accurate, effective communication with patients and their families is critically important. This is a lesson that our health care system must relearn. It is not surprising, for example, that patients and families believe that quality in modern health care demands excellence in communication and nurturing relationships, while many physicians believe that quality of medical care is expressed primarily in terms of biomedical parameters such as cure rates.

Caregivers must understand the patient's and family's beliefs, values, fears, wishes, preferences, and expectations. Thus, those who care for seriously ill patients must learn to listen to their patients attentively and without judgment, with a willingness to be changed by what they hear. In the same manner, readers of the stories contained in the following pages must be willing to be changed by what seriously ill children and their families tell us about what is important to them as they receive treatment in modern health care institutions, enduring a personal struggle to live their lives in the presence of fear, uncertainty, and the constant threat of premature death.

Humans are, by nature, relational beings. Through the words of children facing life-threatening illnesses, we have a greater sense that at the core of our humanity is our basic need for intimate relationships, of having a sense of belonging and order in our lives. Indeed, one of the greatest challenges in our modern health care system is to see human suffering and death not as medical problems, but as life's mysteries to be experienced in a community of intimate relationships.

I vividly remember the words of a 14-year-old boy, Johnny, whom I took care of years ago. His mother, whom he loved dearly, was emotionally fragile and was not coping well with the cancer diagnosis. Johnny and I met to discuss the fact that his cancer, a highly aggressive form of leukemia, had recurred for the second time and was no longer responsive to chemotherapy. After I explained the results of the latest blood tests, Johnny knew that he had only a few days to live. Despite this,

his first question to me was not about himself. Johnny asked, "How is my mother taking all of this?" Rather than returning to his father's home, he then made the decision to stay in the hospital where his mother could receive support from the hospital staff at the time of his death. This relational nature of the illness experience and the healing power of meaningful relationships are palpable in the words of the patients and families presented in this book.

Stories of children with cancer are often stories about a struggle to maintain hope in the face of great adversity. Oddly similar to having an uncertain prognosis, the nature of hope is manifested in expectations of what the future might bring. True hope is always based in the reality of the present situation and helps the person to cope with the threat of uncertainty. A person who loses a leg to cancer, for example, may pray for divine intervention and hope that a new leg will grow back. That person may refuse to learn to walk using a prosthetic device because such action would imply that the hope for a new healthy leg has been lost. However, when hope gives the amputee the courage to engage in rehabilitation, it is no longer merely wishful thinking. Thus, for the patients and families described in the following chapters, the reader can observe their struggle to find a realistic sense of hope that can allow them to have the courage to keep on going, even in the presence of a chronic, life-threatening, or even incurable illness.

These stories of seriously ill children and their families are also passionate narratives about individuals struggling to find purpose and a sense of meaning in their experiences of suffering, serious illness, and possible death. Gloria, the mother of one of my patients, told me years ago that she believed that her teenage son, who was severely impaired from a serious brain injury at the time of birth, experienced the devastating effects of illness so that others could come out of themselves, count their personal blessings, and become better human beings by attending to those in great need. Gloria was not justifying her son's condition; rather, she was expressing a profound sense of purpose and personal meaning she had found in her child's suffering. This deeply spiritual experience, based on the reality of her son's illness, allowed her to have the courage to cope and to even transcend her own personal sufferings. Indeed, the suffering that results from the experience of serious illness and death can be endured and, at times, can be found fulfilling if it is found meaningful.

This constant search for a sense of purpose, this natural and profound need to discover meaning in the misfortunes that life brings, is palpable throughout the pages of this book in the words of patients and family members facing the possibility of a premature death.

Through stories that bring out the paradox of our humanity—joy and suffering mysteriously intertwined —these children and their families communicate to us in no uncertain terms that love and suffering are the fabric of our human existence and are necessarily of great interest to health care professionals involved in caring for the sick. In the richness of their human experiences, we can discover that suffering and death can be transcended when experienced in the context of meaningful, healing relationships.

Javier R. Kane, M.D.
Director, Palliative and End-of-Life Care
St. Jude Children's Research Hospital
Memphis, Tennessee

FROM A PROFESSOR'S PERSPECTIVE

LARRY BROWNING, PH.D.

This book is the outcome of a dissertation that Melody Chatelle wrote as part of the requirements for a Ph. D. in Communication Studies at The University of Texas at Austin. At the planning meeting I had with Melody about the work she wanted to do for her dissertation, I asked her a question that I had never asked another student in my years as a dissertation advisor, but that seemed appropriate for her. I inquired, "Is this taking care of business—in order to get a valuable credential? Or is your dissertation the work of your life?"

The answer to this question was relevant because Melody already had established a successful consulting practice and I wasn't sure what she wanted to accomplish by completing the dissertation. She had performed admirably as a student, but if her goal was to fulfill a requirement to demonstrate competence, then we could work on something that was more manageable and less demanding than the idea she brought to me. Melody wanted to analyze the communication that takes place following the moment a child had been diagnosed with a terminal disease.

Such a heavy topic cannot be taken lightly. No level of effort to get at the heart of this topic is too excessive. Because of her already established consulting career, I did not sense that Melody was preparing to be a pure academic, but she had chosen a topic that was potentially so powerful and provocative that it demanded a commitment to excellence and a nurturing beyond what we usually think of as a task. In addition to the demands of doing this well was the decision concerning what to make of it, once completed. Dissertations are usually written with an eye toward later carving them up and publishing the parts as separate articles to meet the publishing requirements for beginning an individual's academic career. The problem of how to present the data came up again. It wasn't clear how to both summarize and aggregate the data and yet leave all the stories intact. Melody's biggest commitment was to the integrity of each story. The presentation of her research in book form means she was able to honor all the stories and leave the thoughts about impact to the reader.

I had never asked the question about a dissertation being a "life's work" before. The inquiry was so pointed that I worried that I would get a politically correct rather than a candid answer. But without hesitation, Melody answered, "This is the work of my life." From that moment on, that was my criterion for being a guide and helper: Keep Melody focused on the work of her life; the steps Melody took to write this book are the evidence of the truth of that statement.

She took on the requirement of locating parents and children who were in these sad and tragic circumstances and asked them for permission to share the difficult and private times associated with the diagnosis of a disease; she took the audio tapes with doctors, family members, and children that she collected and had them transcribed. Melody then listened to her tapes while reading the transcripts to make certain that the data matched what she heard in the interviews.

After Melody completed transcribing the tapes, I read them in preparation for discussions about how to present them in the best way. Two things stood out to me: first, the poignancy and depth of the interviews she had collected was so strong that they had to be consumed in bits, so I read about thirty pages per day until I had completed a review of her raw data; second, after reading the transcripts of the interviews, I was uncertain whether we should meet in my office to talk about writing details or in a chapel to ask for spiritual guidance in handling these reverent materials.

Though we met in my office, our sense that this was special material requiring special handling was tacitly understood. This feeling of reverence stayed with us throughout the project, which resulted in emphasizing each story individually. Rather than grouping the stories to see how much we could gain from a comparative analysis, we decided that each child's experience was so distinct that a separate chapter and analysis for each person was necessary.

The chapters you see in this book are the outcomes of Melody's work. These stories are polyvocal; your understanding of them can be scattered among the tiniest detail in any of these accounts. I invite you to engage them with the caring and consideration with which they were written.

Larry Browning, Ph.D.
Professor, The University of Texas at Austin
College of Communication Studies
Austin, Texas

Memories are a gift of the past,
That we hold in the present,
To create what can be a great future.
Treasure and keep memories,
For the sake of Life.
Mattie J. T. Stepanek, Author

THE AUTHOR'S PERSPECTIVE:
MY OWN JOURNEY

Everyone has stories of profound influence and impact. My own personal journey led me to an intense desire to know more about death and dying, most especially the deaths of children and young people.

Within a 12-day period, I had the privilege of sitting next to two women as they took their last breaths. The two women were mother and daughter. Together they represented two of the most important women in my own personal life, my own 72-year-old mother, Irma Jeanne Chatelle, and her mother, my 95-year-old grandmother, Faye Farley.

Until age 42, I had never seen anyone actually die. Nor had I ever held the hands of someone as he or she breathed a last breath, and then waited to see if anything else happened. Never before had I looked at a medical professional and said through my tears, "Is she actually dead now?" Nor had I ever helped funeral home professionals put a person in a body bag. Without a doubt, the deaths, and the lives of those two remarkable women, changed my life.

One of the deaths was expected, that of my beloved 72-year-old mother. She had battled cancer intermittently for 17 years with a strong will, unimaginable perseverance, a heart of gold, and the gift of humor until

1

the bitter end. She used to tell my father he was going to be very popular with the ladies after she died because he was one of the few "old men" in their small hometown who could drive at night. After undergoing her second mastectomy, she would laugh and say, "Thank God that God didn't give women three breasts." (In deference to my mother's love for, and delight in using, raw humor, a note must be made in her honor that she did not always use the more civilized word *breasts*.) Later upon being diagnosed with lung cancer despite having quit smoking more than thirty years prior, she would say with a sad and ironic smile, "Perhaps I spoke too soon."

We were first told in August that my mother would most likely die then. She did not. She held on to soak up many more days of going to garage sales, winning a few more hands of poker, telling jokes, spending time with her beloved granddaughters, celebrating her 72nd birthday, and living through, albeit in a very bad physical state, one last Thanksgiving.

At first my father, sister, and I would together sit with my mother just to be near her because she was always the life of the party, and we knew the party would soon be coming to an end. We would tell jokes, play cards, remember stories, create beanie-baby puppet shows with my nieces, laugh at stupid things on television, listen to music, and so on. Yet as the days and weeks turned into months during which my mother steadily declined, no longer could our own stamina or schedules sustain a group vigil for 24 hours a day. Thus we began taking turns.

My mother passed away on November 30, three months after she was initially expected to die. In what appeared to be another "routine" evening of hand holding, touching, and monitoring her breathing, I whispered to my mother, who was comatose at the time, that Dad was going out for a quick walk around the block, and that he would be right back. No sooner had my dad left the house and shut the door behind him before there was a change in my mother's labored breathing. Although this had happened before, something seemed different this time. Mom's breathing seemed thinner than usual.

I did not know whether to stay or leave my mother and run after my dad, but I was afraid that my mother might die alone. So I stayed and continued to hold her hand and tell her everything would be fine, hoping for so many reasons that Dad would walk back in the door.

Throughout the next several minutes, I thought to myself how clueless I felt in terms of what to try to say to my mom through my tears, even though I had poured through a stack of books on how to care for the dying. All I could seem to spit out was, "I love you, we'll take care of each other here, we'll see you again, it's okay to let go if you want to, and everything will be fine." In a few minutes, my mother took one last stutter of a breath. As I continued to hold her hand, my eyes went back and forth from her contorted face to the ticking of the clock to see if anything else would happen. Nothing did. After five or more minutes had passed, I knew it was probably really over this time.

A few minutes later, my dad returned. When he came into the room, I told him I thought Mom had died. We both held her hands for a long time to see together if it really was over. Then I quietly stepped out of the room to give Dad some time alone with Mom. I went to call my sister.

Unlike my mother, my grandmother's death 12 days before had been entirely unexpected despite her age. My grandmother was in excellent shape for a 95 year old, although she had been sitting in her nursing home room for several weeks fretting about my mother's health. Yet always before, my mother managed to get better even after having both breast cancer and lung cancer twice. No doubt my grandmother was hoping and praying for yet another miracle from and for her grown daughter. We all were.

When we went to tell my grandmother that most likely my mother would not survive this "bout" with cancer, she looked straight at me and emphatically said, "I do not want to be here to watch one of my girls die." We all told her how badly we felt about everything. I made arrangements to pick her up the next morning to take her to visit Mom for perhaps the last time. As we left my grandmother, we asked to have a social worker look in on her periodically because she was really sad.

Later that afternoon, the nursing home staff called. They said my grandmother had somehow broken her hip and was beginning to slip into a coma that would likely kill her. No one had seen her fall, nor would she ever tell us if she had fallen. We were incredulous. I went to be with her at the nursing home. When I asked her if she were somehow making herself sick because of Mom, she just smiled slightly and remained quiet.

Later that evening my grandmother died. After a several hour period, her breaths simply became more shallow and distanced in time. At the very end she took one last little breath, and then nothing else. She and I were the only two people in her room. A nurse's aide came in a little while later to check on us. I asked her if my grandmother was dead. She nodded.

The nurse's aide then asked me if she could spend some time alone with my grandmother. I did not know what she intended to do, but I knew I needed to call my family, so I stepped outside the room. When I walked back into my grandmother's room, my silver-haired precious grandmother lay there with her eyes shut in a fresh new nightgown and robe. Her hands were folded across her stomach. She lay on top of fresh bed linens.

My grandmother looked absolutely beautiful, just like a 95-year-old Sleeping Beauty. Her body was full of grace and poise. To this day I will always be indebted to that nurse's aide. She had changed the bedsheets and fully bathed and redressed a dead person. Maybe that was nursing home protocol. To me it was amazing grace from a guardian angel saint.

As we waited together for the funeral home personnel to arrive, the aide stayed with me as I brushed my grandmother's hair and told her stories about this wonderful woman. When the funeral directors arrived, I helped them place my grandmother into a body bag, something I could not later bring myself to do with my mother.

We then walked quietly and slowly down the long nursing home corridor. There were four of us: myself, two people from the funeral home, and my grandmother in a body bag on a gurney. As we walked down the corridor, I saw several elderly residents standing quietly at their doors, almost as if to pay their last respects. I thought to myself how hard it must be when you are elderly to see one of your fellow nursing home residents being taken out in a body bag. I was extremely sad for them and sad for us.

To this day there are so many unanswered questions remaining in my mind about death, despite having watched two very significant people in my life die. I wonder how people truly make sense of their own losses. I wonder how people cope and carry on after losing entire families in one quick second because of accidents. I continue to think about the massive and tragic loss from the September 11th tragedy in which terrorists attacked the Twin Towers at the World Trade Center via hijacked airplanes.

Amidst all of the uncertainties of life and death alike, what I do know is that my grandmother's death helped prepare me for my mother's death 12 days later. It also was a stark personal revelation to me that losing a child, even a child the age of my mother, is just not the way it is supposed to happen.

As I sat at the funerals for my grandmother and then my mother, I began my own personal journey into thinking and wondering about death. I was moved by the thought about the unconditional love of a mother (or father) for one's children, and the dire need to avoid the pain of losing a child. I began to think how we as a family might have felt even more consumed with grief, if that were possible, had the caskets been smaller and contained the remains of younger members of our family. The thoughts and questions stayed with me long after the funerals ended. Thus began the learning journey that continues to this day.

Stories and Conversations

Author's note—Use of pseudonyms

For privacy purposes, pseudonyms are used throughout *Journeys of Heartache and Grace* except as noted. In Chapter 1, the beginning story entitled Minister David Foretells, David's real name is David Barrera. In Chapter 4 entitled Praising Life, the Ede family's name and web site are used with permission.

In most other cases, names and details of the young people, their medical caregivers and personal histories, and family members have been changed to protect their privacy as well as those around them.

Statistics referenced in the individual stories are reflective of 2004 data at the time the stories were initially shared by the respondents.

Stories are messages that unfold naturally.
They give coherence to a group subculture.
Dr. Larry Browning,
Communication Scholar

SETTING THE STAGE: THE STORIES

In the spring of 2004, a handsome 13-year-old boy named David Barrera of San Antonio, Texas was laid to rest after a 12-year struggle with spinal muscular atrophy. The disease also killed his younger brother at the age of four. Despite his boyish grin and youthful heart, David faced his disease head on and asked others to do the same for him: to speak the truth about his situation. At the same time, he used his illness as a way to connect with the people in his world. He was appointed a Minister of Christ with the Storehouse Ministry Fellowship and told his story to anyone who would listen in order to leave a legacy of goodwill and enlightenment for humanity. I was privileged to have the opportunity to listen.

David is not unique. Other young people have remarkable stories to tell about dying in an honest and straightforward way. And they want us all to listen.

One of the most mysterious, confusing, and unexamined times in all our lives is right before death. People can talk at length *about* a person who is facing a terminal or advanced illness and the particulars of the medical prognoses. Yet when the time comes to talking directly *with* such a person, we are often stymied, even around those closest to us. Time and time again during end-of-life situations, people say:

9

"I don't know what to say to my friend who is dying";

"I'm afraid I'll say the wrong thing and make matters worse";

"What if my spouse hears the word 'death'?";

"Talking is just too hard right now, so I'm going to stay away"; or

"I am emotionally sad, and it can't be helpful to see a person continually crying."

The list of reasons to avoid one of life's most important periods seems endless.

Communication experts say that talking about death with people who are known to be dying represents perhaps the biggest communication challenge we will face at some point in our lives. Despite the inevitability of death, help is noticeably scarce.

Journeys of Heartache and Grace represents a compilation of wonderfully rich and powerful stories of 13 young people who want to help us learn and be truly present with dying loved ones by telling their own stories and sharing advice. Most of them actively accepted the reality that they were dying, some sooner than others.

As we care for aging parents, have serious illnesses ourselves, or face the unthinkable prospect of a dying child in our own families, *Journeys of Heartache and Grace* can help us improve our communication and stay more connected. Perhaps it can help make the last days with those we love more meaningful.

-1-

MINISTER DAVID FORETELLS

In a small apartment complex in San Antonio, Texas, a young man named David, affectionately known as Minister David, sat close to the front door in his wheelchair waiting for me to step inside. The young man and his mother were anxious to tell me of their lives in the spirit of witnessing. Their story began with Minister David's vision of his brother, Eddie, who had died several years earlier. Minister David told me about seeing his late brother, declaring in a biblical tone and lyrical tempo: "My brothers and sisters in Christ, I bring you good news of great joy. For I have seen a great light. And the great light is that of my brother, Little Eddie."

David remembers seeing his four-year-old brother quite clearly, a brother who died of the same disease that is slowly killing David. What is curious about the vision is that no one in the family had talked very much with David about Little Eddie. Everyone wanted to spare David such vivid reminders of the illness they shared and its possible fatalistic outcomes.

Despite dying so young, Little Eddie seems to have paved much of the way for his brother. Little Eddie was treated in a small community where medical technology and innovation at the time were quite limited.

"[There] they didn't have the technology like we have now, like the IPV machine, the VPAP machine, they didn't have all that," David explained. The Intra-pulmonary percussive ventilation (IPV(r)) machine helps clear individuals' lungs and improve overall breathing. The variable positive airway pressure (VPAP(r)) machine is designed to help with breathing overall and specifically to assist in alerting patients and caregivers when respiratory pressure is too high, too low, or there is a power failure involving any of the breathing assistance machines.

David's vision of Little Eddie gave him the impetus to insist that a move be made across Texas. He wanted to be near a large hospital serving pediatric residents where physicians were learning more and more about his disease. The move from a small community to a metropolitan area also helped David solve family issues, primarily for his mom.

"I just kept telling Mom that we have to move away and that the smaller town is a trap, and we need to get out of there." David was saddened that his dad's actions showed he did not want to work things out with his family because of medical and financial issues involv-ing his son. "I just kept telling Mom over and over again that we have to go to the bigger place. It's a trap, and we need to get out of there."

After the move, when David's father sent his mom divorce papers saying their marriage was nothing more than "a big show," David responded by encouraging his mom and viewing the dilemma as a mother/son partnership problem, saying "*we* had to go through that part, and *we* got through it." David continued to be estranged from his father. "Up until now, ever since we left the house to come down here to San Antonio, I haven't seen him ever since. I don't want no contact. I don't want to, I don't. . . . I don't really want contact with him because I don't want him to give my mom trouble."

In the particular vision David remembers, Little Eddie visited him when David was hospitalized again because of his disease. David describes the encounter:

"Little Eddie came. I saw him in a vision with two other angels. I didn't know who they were. I couldn't really visualize them. But he had come and he told me: 'Get Mom out of there. It's a trap.'"

So David insisted that he and his mother leave Alamo, which had been their home, in order to receive better medical care and escape worrisome family problems, both of which became a reality.

David spends his days sitting in a wheelchair. A special transport van picks him up in the early hours of the morning and takes him to school. His nights are spent sleeping on a small hospital-type bed tethered to oxygen.

David has been stricken with neuro-muscular-dystrophy (NMD), or more specifically, spinal muscular atrophy (SMA). Spinal muscular atrophy is a genetic mutation destroying nerve cells in the spinal cord, leading to muscle weakness and atrophy (wasting). For David, the disease has specifically robbed him of his ability to walk, and so he transfers from his hospital bed to a wheelchair, relies heavily on oxygen, and is surrounded by machines to help him maneuver through the day. When not attending school, David spends most of his time playing video games, watching television, talking to friends who call him "Dude," and visiting with his mother and grandmother. Amidst the many celebrity posters and computer games, David's bedroom looks like a mini-hospital ward.

Twelve years ago, physicians told David's mother he would not live to his first birthday because of his physical plight. Today he defiantly contorts his body and thrusts a clenched fist in the air from his wheelchair to proclaim his longevity at age 12. "Against all odds" seems a fitting mantra for David, especially as compared to the very short life of his brother. On a spiritual note, when asked if God talks back to David, he responded without looking up and without elaboration, "Yeah."

Carrying on an extended conversation with David means sometimes you are talking with a typical 12-year-old boy whose favorite movie is *Finding Nemo* and who blushes when he talks about meeting a beauty contestant winner from San Antonio. At other times, talking with this child with a disability means you are receiving The Word from Minister David. He is quick to quote Bible verses. He sings his praise to God and his people as a soloist at his church where he prays for all the people of his beloved Rio Grande Valley, San Antonio, and surrounding cities. He also actively solicits food and toy donations for the underserved, all as callings from God.

Both David and his mom wholeheartedly feel that David has lived 11 years longer than expected for a variety of reasons, including the love and care of outstanding physicians and the benefit of research and technology surrounding him in San Antonio. Yet the primary reason David believes he is still alive is because God has called him to minister to others. This special calling has allowed, and mandated, that David live in order to become Minister David and be of service and outreach to others. God "helps me out," David explained, thus repaying debts to society via community service is important to him.

David defines this outreach as his "legacy," a word that many 12-year-old boys could arguably not even know, much less feel a burning desire to create before they die. David likes to tell his story over and over again so that he can sustain his legacy as fast as he can because of his limited life expectancy.

During the Christmas season, Minister David actively solicits funds in order to dress up in his Christmas colored tuxedo with a Santa hat with bells in order to hand out toys to younger children who are less fortunate. When asked how his legacy building was proceeding, he replied: "Oh, it's going good. I still haven't reached as many as I had over there in Alamo. We are still getting our feet wet here. We're still trying to get more people here in San Antonio."

David wants to make others understand how to relate to people like him. He wants people to understand that having a disability does not make one less of a person and that there is a great difference between "people" and "animals."

"I like it when people treat people with disabilities as people—like regular people. Because we are; we're not just animals; we're not anything like that. We're normal human beings. We are just like any normal person."

David firmly believes that "even though we do come in different shapes and sizes and colors and everything, we're just like everybody else. It's no different; the bottom line is that we're still human beings."

One of David's favorite people is his physician, Dr. Morse. They love each other, and David's face lights up with a smile when anyone mentions her name. David loves to talk about her and tell stories of how they work together to keep him from dying.

Dr. Morse is well known in San Antonio for her work with young people and children. After years of medical practice as a pediatric pulmonary specialist, she says only now has she learned to love and lose a patient and survive and "be better for it."

Together Dr. Morse and David fix his lungs, for the time being, over and over and over again. Like so many young people with spinal muscular atrophy, David repeatedly finds himself knocking at death's door because of lung fluid problems. Dr. Morse has repeatedly saved him. They work together as a team, and they "shoot straight" with each other about the severity of each occurrence.

"We openly speak of him dying sooner rather than later, although unlike cancer there is no timetable," Dr. Morse said. "As long as he doesn't get an infection, he can go on a while; but when he gets a cold, he just goes downhill," she added.

During a particularly difficult time one year, Dr. Morse repeatedly tried to eliminate fluid from David's lungs so that he could breathe, but without complete success.

"Dr. Morse told my mom to prepare for the worst and to start thinking reality," David said. Prior to the fifth or sixth procedure, David had told his mom that he wasn't ready to die yet, although he knew that Dr. Morse had tried everything humanly possible to clean out his lungs. He even told Dr. Morse before the procedure took place not to feel badly if it didn't work this time because she had tried so hard.

He also specifically called Dr. Morse over to his hospital gurney before the procedure to say thank you to her for all of her efforts.

"I want to thank you, and I know you have done and you are doing everything in your power that you can, and I want to tell you that I love you," David told Dr. Morse. "I saw my mom turn around, and she started to cry. Dr. Morse put her head down, and she turned red. I saw her," David remembered. He specifically requested that Dr. Morse watch over his mother because he knew that she would be sad when he died.

"And finally it came to Dr. Morse, and God gave her this idea," David said explaining an innovative air-blowing procedure that Dr. Morse had created specifically for him as a last-ditch attempt to keep him alive. When the procedure ended, Minister David said, "Dr. Morse, God gave you the grace and the knowledge and the power to get through this.'"

David believes talking about his illness is a way of helping others. When asked if Dr. Morse always "shoots straight" with him, he replied, "Yes. She's a really good doctor, and I have a really good relationship with her."

Talking directly is important to both David and his mom. David's mom affectionately remembers the time when he told another doctor, "You know what? This is my body. You are going to do the things to my body. So you speak to me." He was 11 or 12 years old at the time.

"Sometimes I tell other people about my illness, and I think it sort of helps them to understand," David said. "I say to them: Oh, it's OK, it's not really that bad."

David especially prefers to hear directly from all his doctors, as opposed to some physicians' practice of asking the parents to first step outside the room for conversation, leaving the young patients alone to wonder what is being said about them. David despises this outside-the-room dialogue practice that he again likens to inhumane treatment of the less than human. "I tell people that I don't like people who treat us like animals," he stated.

A mother's perspective

Being honest and straightforward with David has become important to David's mother, Diana. Yet as a mother, she first tried to protect her younger son from thinking about death. She did not talk with David about Little Eddie because of the disease they shared. When David told her he already knew about Little Eddie from his vision in the hospital, communication lines between Diana and her son were strengthened even more.

"I thought David wasn't ready to know of his brother and why he had passed on," Diana commented. "Then David told me he had spoken to Little Eddie. It was at that time that David knew and understood what was going on. It was through that experience that he started being more open and also talking about if he himself were to pass on. We are very open about dying."

Diana also told another prophetic story in which David somehow learned of the death of a friend who was a Catholic nun long before the news was actually delivered to the family by a minister. As the story goes, David was in the hospital and had asked to be taken outside for some fresh air and to look at the buildings. While he and Diana were sitting outside, they saw an eagle soaring. Diana felt an overwhelming peace fill her heart and soul.

"I know about coming under the shadows of the Almighty and that His wings will cover us," she said.

After seeing the eagle, both David and Diana then saw a dove fly by and sit on a window ledge. The dove began staring at the two of them.

"And then David says to me, 'You know, Mom, this is no coincidence,'" referring to seeing the eagle and the dove. "'There is a message behind this.' Then David says to me, 'Do you remember the sister from church? The sister passed away already.'"

Later that day when the parish priest called to check on David, Diana asked about the sister. Actually, she commented to the pastor that she already knew the sister had died. The pastor asked Diana how she had become aware of that situation. She answered, "David told me."

To this day, both David and Diana believe that the sister sent the eagle and the dove to appear to them in the hospital garden so that together they might pray for the sister as she made her transition from earthly life to death. They cherish that memory.

Diana believes she and David have a natural and a spiritual understanding that will sustain them both, regardless of the future. She affirms that as David grows older, he should become more of an advocate for his own needs.

No longer will Diana allow physicians to pull her aside to talk separately from David about her son's grave medical situation.

"David, I don't need to teach you any more. You are an advocate on your own," Diana said. Slowly she is beginning to release her son, just as she had to do with

Little Eddie. Despite relying fully on God, sometimes her faith waivers, given that both of her children were born with the same fatal disease.

"It's not to say I don't feel the anger or. . . say, *Why me?* Because those questions do come, and those feelings do come," Diana explained. "However, I know that I am not in control of our lives, and I know that our lives are only passing through here. I know that I need to trust and depend on the Lord."

Diana lives for the moment. She fully accepts that only through God's grace will she be able to handle what is yet to come her way. For now, she wants and needs to live each day in the moment, knowing that, as the saying goes, tomorrow will be another day.

"Staying still" is the bottom line for Diana. "Sometimes things are so challenging. Life is so challenging and hard, not knowing about the unknown. We need to know that if we are emotionally reacting to the situation, then we need to stay still, and the answer will come. In the meantime, each day is God's masterpiece."

Like so many sages before him who have lived much longer lives, David has visions about his life as it stands today and his future. He still continues a relationship with Little Eddie through his dreams. Little Eddie would be 16 now if he were still alive. Perhaps the brothers are preparing for a reunion in a different realm.

David continues to talk with his mom about his illness. Most of the time, however, they prefer to just go about "enjoying their lives, enjoying God together," David said. "We usually do things together, like eat and we play games."

Yet the notion of life and death is still fraught with high stakes and weariness for David and his mom. Sometimes talking or thinking about the future is difficult for David. When I asked him a question about his future he said, "Sounds like it's going to rain or something."

Nonetheless, perhaps talking about the future is something David chooses not to do, as opposed to avoiding the topic entirely. Like the angel Gabriel in the Christmas story who foretells the coming of a special birth, David seems to know how things are going to turn out in terms of his own life and death story. At age 12, he appears not to be unfolding his entire life story. He does, however, seem to gingerly suggest a premonition:

> "Well, there's some stuff coming in the future. Next year, I don't know the whole story. Only God knows what's in store for me next year. Yeah, there are things coming in the future, probably this month or next month. It will be quite a few weeks from now. I'm just praying about it," he confided.

With that, David begins to sing Christian songs with full vibrato, using his much-coveted lungs to praise his God. His mom joins in. Together they make beautiful harmony.

"Against all odds." That is The Word proclaimed through the life being led by 12-year-old Minister David.

Epilogue

Five months later, Minister David's mother called to say that David was in the hospital and not doing well. The last time I saw him, he was about half the size as before. The circumference of his arms and legs was about the size of a quarter. He could barely say hello, much less sing. He smiled slightly when I walked into the room.

While David rested, his mother walked me around the hospital wing. She showed me the Tree of Life plaque commemorating those children who died within the previous few years. Each child had a bronze square with his or her name engraved on it, signifying the branches of the tree. About one-half of the squares were blank.

Diana pointed to the bronze square at the very top of the tree: "That's the one David picked out for himself when we arrived here at the hospital a few days ago," she said.

A few days after our visit, David was discharged from the hospital to die at home. Before he was released, David fulfilled his dream of giving his mom a surprise birthday party in his hospital room. His other dream was to meet San Antonio Spurs basketball star David Robinson. Mr. Robinson said afterwards that this special 12-year-old minister meant more to him than anyone he had ever met, according to David's mom.

Three weeks later on an early Saturday morning, David asked his mom to physically lift him up in bed so that he could reach out to God and the angels. He was ready to go. He died a few minutes later, telling his mom with his last breath that he loved her. The local newspaper ran a story about his death and his ministries.

At his funeral, the 12-year-old boy/minister looked handsome and distinguished. He was lying in a silver casket clothed in a black tux, complete with cummerbund and bowtie. People spoke of a reality in which this young man was simply running a race ahead of his time.

His beloved Dr. Morse gave one of the many eulogies. She remembered a time when she had to lobby David hard to wear an oxygen mask at night so that his lungs could rest. Finally she told David that if he wore the mask, he would be like an astronaut who could fly to the moon at night. The next time he saw her, he told her that her ploy had worked. He had worn the mask and been to the moon—and that the moon was indeed made of cheese.

In true form, David had the last written and spoken word at his own funeral. The funeral program contained a message from him shown below verbatim, in his unique style of writing and punctuation:

> Thank you for spending this special day with me for the laughter and memories this day will bring I thank my dear lord for the blessings like you and I hope that in time, you'll reminisce of this day and say to yourself, "Oh, what a glorious time."

At the end of the service, his aunt played a cassette tape of Minister David speaking in a clear, firm voice: "Bye, everybody. I shall miss you all."

Eulogy by Martha Morse, M.D.
For David Barrera 4/28/91-3/6/04

I have been in medicine for half my life now. I have been touched and taught by many patients and families. ... It is love for my patients that keeps me going. David Barrera and his mother Diana are part of my Barnabas group, the group that encourages me. I have come here tonight to celebrate David's life and to give thanks to David and Diana for what they have contributed to my life.

I met David in October of 1995 when he was four years old. David, like his older brother, was diagnosed with Spinal Muscular Atrophy. Some people, who didn't know David very well, might have thought that David's life was terrible and not worth living. ...But, the David I knew saw his life as one worth living. In fact, he told me a few months ago, that he still had some things he needed to finish doing before he died.

I watched David grow up in the eight and a half years I knew him....David was a "people" person – a trait I am sure he gets from his mom. ...David was gifted with a beautiful singing voice, as is his mother. And he and Diana made beautiful music together. Even in the last few months, when David was so weak he could hardly open his mouth, somehow he could still sing like an angel. Diana looked for ways to help David share his gift with others....Over the years, David would come into my office and I would ask him to sing. Sometimes I needed the lift—sometimes my staff needed a reminder of why we do what we do. But there was one time when I asked David to sing to one of my patients about his same age. Eric was also confined to a wheelchair, unable to move, and unable to talk. I asked David if he would sing Eric a song. And of course, David did—a song about angels flying so close to the ground that they clipped their wings. Eric broke out in a huge smile. David had connected with him. It was one of those "holy moments."

David was well named. He was a man after God's own heart. One time when he was in the hospital recovering from yet another bout of pneumonia in his collapsed lung, I was going to have to leave him for a week to the care of a colleague. My husband and I had planned a vacation to the Yucatán. I remember my last day before vacation. David asked if he could pray for me. We held hands and he prayed quite a long prayer that involved my safety and that of my husband. I remember there was a line in there about God sending thousands of angels to bear us up should we fall. As I sat at the bottom of the pyramid at Chichen Itza watching my husband climb it, I reminded God of David's prayer.

Over the past year, David began to grow weaker. We began to talk more seriously about choices. I was no longer talking to a child who was scared of more medical procedures. I was talking to a bright, insightful young man who knew his own mind. God granted us another six months. And David began to prepare for his death. When David came to our office in December, he asked his mother to leave the room so he could talk to me privately. This was certainly a first!.... David wanted us to have a party for his mom. Her birthday was past, but that didn't matter to him. He wanted balloons and a chocolate cake. We put the date on the schedule for February and kept mum.

During David's last hospitalization, he reminded me of that surprise birthday party he wanted to give for his mother. He felt that the time had come. Everyone from Child Life went into high gear. The purple balloons, the chocolate cake, a mold of his hands, a bracelet with purple hearts and an angel with gold wings were all to be a part of this. On the day of the party, David awoke early and kept insisting that his mom get him up and get him going. Diana, not knowing what was happening, was just not moving fast enough to suit him. But he persisted and talked her into showing him the "Room Above the Clouds" where children and their parents may go when they are dying.

He picked out the spot on the bronze tree that would bear the leaf with his name on it after he died. And then he was ready; people were spilling out of the playroom, trying to hide and not give the party away, but it could be hidden no more. Diana was overwhelmed at this Mother's Appreciation Party. David was just beaming. Many came to honor Diana who had given her son not only life but also a life worth living.

David never returned to our office. During his last hospitalization, we talked about his life on this earth growing short. David became very tearful. I tried to explore with him what he was feeling. He denied that his tears had to do with fear of any suffering he might face. He denied being afraid to die. He said he knew he would be with Jesus. His tears, as it turned out, were about leaving his mother behind. Who would care for her?

During our visit, I asked David where he wanted to die and what he wanted at his funeral. He decided that though the Cloud Room was beautiful, he wanted to go home to die. He began to work on his funeral. He wanted us all to be happy and celebrate. I told him that we could be happy for him, but if we cried it was because we were missing him.

David had one more thing he wanted to accomplish in life before he died. David had met many many dignitaries and had sung in many, many public places, but he just wanted to meet "THE MAN." A couple of hours later, "THE MAN" (San Antonio Spurs star) came and met David. I don't know whether David Robinson or David Barrera was blessed more by the occasion. I know that David Barrera was not disappointed. He met the man he had placed on a pedestal – he stood tall and he did not fall!

As a physician, I am frequently around death. There have been times in my life when I have struggled very much with the question of "why does a loving God allow such suffering in the world?" Some people are able to just resign themselves to believing that it is God's will and we should not question. Other people just get angry and don't believe there is a personal, loving God. Other people claim to have it all figured out and have all the answers. None of these work for me. But perhaps there is another way of thinking. Perhaps it is that life is a gift – pure, simple, sheer gift – and that we here on earth are to relate to it accordingly.

I saw David about three days before he died. He looked very weak and pale. I held his hand and he smiled at me. Above his bed was a picture of the Spurs winning the championship. And below it is the picture of the two of us doing the children's sermon. David assured me that he was comfortable at home. I asked him if he was having any dreams. He smiled and said, "beautiful ones." He told me of seeing Jesus—that heaven was indeed made of gold. He told me of seeing Paul, also one of my special patients who died at Thanksgiving. David wanted me to know that Paul was "very, very happy." He told me of seeing his brother, Little Eddie, but he couldn't quite make out his face.

Tonight we look at David's life and David's death and some of us may scream "*why*?" David was a gift to us pure and simple. I loved him, so I miss him and I hurt, but I am grateful for having gotten to be a part of his life for eight and a half years.

Why did he have to suffer and die? None of us will totally be able to answer that question, yet I know that God did not even spare his own son from suffering and death—and I know that God has prepared a wonderful place for David and us when we die. Perhaps, David was seeing it as he began to shout as he was dying, "pull me up, pull me up!"

Martha Morse, M.D.
A Portion of her Eulogy (With permission)
March 11, 2004

Minister David Foretells
An Interviewer's Perspective

A Lesson Learned - *Knowing*

From the minute I met David at the front door of his San Antonio apartment, his face and story became embedded in my memory. Indeed this little boy fulfilled his mission of creating in me a lasting legacy of his wonderful spirit and soul.

One of the greatest lessons learned from Minister David's story centers around the theme of *knowing*. Think about all of the funerals you may have attended in your lifetime. Have you ever read a personally-written note in the bulletin or heard a pre-recorded taped message from the deceased? Never before had this happened to me; and certainly it was completely unexpected behavior from a 12-year-old boy.

Yet David knew. He knew that he was going to die way too soon. He knew that parts of his legacy would be left undone or left for others, like his mother, to carry on. David also knew the way he wanted things to be prior to his death. He was completely clear that he wanted to be treated just like other people. He wanted to create and sustain his own destiny, with little fanfare for his physical illness. He wanted to carry out God's mission until the end – and then keep going through his legacy, just as his little brother Eddie said he would do.

Suggested Response Strategies/Discussion Questions/ Commentary:

** Children and young people like David teach us a great deal about our own deaths at any age and the deaths of those we love, including the reality that at some level most people *know* what is happening to them and what the future holds. Thus end-of-life times and interactions with others should be based on perceptions of *knowing* rather than *avoiding*. Death should not become the proverbial elephant in the room that everyone avoids talking about. Instead, take your cues from the person who is seriously ill and / or dying.

** Ask questions like:
> *-How are you feeling today?*
> *-What kind of a day are you having today?*
> *-We both know that you are really sick. Are there some things I can do for you to ease your mind in any way about the future?*

** Think about your own legacy after you die. Like David, what do you want to leave behind? Is there a certain way you want your obituary to be written? How do you want your funeral to be conducted? Is there a message you want to leave behind or tell someone before you die? Are there loose ends you need to handle before you die to help you and others in your life?

Your Personal Notes/Action Steps:

-2-

THE HOOTERS GUY

For his 16th birthday in the fall of 2003, Richard wanted to go to a place called Hooters, a restaurant chain known for its physically-endowed and scantily-clad waitresses. And that he did—wheelchair and oxygen and all—along with his mom and his beloved hospice friends who cared for him. The entourage even included the hospice chaplain, Reverend Jeanne, as Richard called her. Reverend Jeanne proclaimed the outing as a "monumental and joyful and wonderful celebration of life."

A short time later Richard's mom sent me the following email: "I just wanted to let you know that Richard went home to be with his Lord yesterday morning."

Richard's story

Richard embraced life with a smile that rippled off the sides of his face and down his thin body like water from an edgeless swimming pool. He laughed at the humor, or attempted humor, of others around him almost as much as he laughed at himself.

Life, for Richard, was ridiculously funny, embarrassing, joyful, and full of love. Yet life was quickly slipping away. He died less than eight weeks after this interview was conducted, a little more than one month after his 16th birthday celebration at Hooters.

Richard was born with ataxia-telangiectasia (A-T), but did not officially receive the diagnosis until he was 11 years old. A-T is a progressive, degenerative illness that attacks many body systems. According to the A-T Children's Project, children with this disease usually appear "normal" at birth, yet begin showing signs of the disease in the second year of life. Initial signs may include slurred speech stemming from a lack of muscle control called "ataxia" and "wobbly" balance.

After the onset of ataxia, usually tiny red spider veins called telangiectasia appear on the surface of the ears and cheeks or corners of the eyes exposed to sunlight. Approximately 70 percent of children also experience recurrent and possibly life-threatening respiratory infections.

Richard nearly died several times during his 16 years of life. Yet he kept bouncing back. He never failed to see the irony or humor of the situation. During my visit, this frank exchange took place.

Richard's mom to Richard: "Do you want to say what the doctor told you who put you in hospice?"

Richard: "Yeah. I had six months."

Interviewer: "Six months to live? How long ago was that?"

Richard: "Six years ago." (A huge smile engulfs Richard's face.) He quickly added, "And I'm still here."

Richard led a full and active life during his short life. He loved to watch football on television. He loved to bowl, and he believed he was a "darn good bowler" who loved to throw strikes. He loved to go to the Special Olympics, where he competed in the softball throw. He was good at throwing the ball. He loved the movie *Star Wars*. The small bathroom he shared with his brother and mom was covered with movie paraphernalia and posters of Luke Skywalker in action.

Richard's body may have been physically challenged, but his ego was healthy. He was proud to have been featured in a newspaper article about his own physician and her work with young people.

Richard would happily, yet sheepishly, grin when you showed him a copy of the newspaper article. He would then scribble an illegible "autograph" that he said was his name on your copy. Before he returned it to you, he would ask you to give him some dollars or at least some spare change. He seemed like the proverbial and lovable con man. In this case, the con man was a teenage boy sitting contorted in his wheelchair with a twinkle in his eye, a smile that would not quit, and a bottomless heart of gold.

Despite his positive countenance and brilliant sense of humor, Richard did not like being noticeably sick. He did not want people to know when he was getting oxygen, and he fought the physical progressions of his disease to the bitter end.

His mom said Richard's need to use a wheelchair came all of a sudden, as if he had willed his legs to hold him up for as long as he could. The same was true for other medical necessities.

"He never had a feeding tube, a G (gastrointestinal) tube, and (all of a sudden) he had to have one of those. And we never had to have nursing care before, and now we're going to have to," his mom explained. In Richard's house, things seemed to be one way for the 16 year old for one minute and then a completely different way the next.

When Richard was forced to use oxygen, he oftentimes refused to go to school or church. Before he died, he often asked one of his hospice workers how many more times she thought he would have to be on oxygen, because "there are times when he thinks that he will no longer bounce back from being on oxygen or antibiotics," his mom said.

Although the oxygen tubes going into his nose gave him the breathing assistance he desperately needed to stay alive, they made Richard feel horribly embarrassed and self-conscious. Interestingly enough, Richard lived in modern western civilization where body piercing and tattoos over all parts of the body seem to be a relatively typical and prevalent sign of individuality, if not popularity. Yet for Richard, somehow the removable, clear, and noiseless tubes that were unnoticeable to the adults around him became like a giant noose around his neck that shouted out in neon colors: "Warning: Different in a Bad Way!" Richard wanted no part of being different.

Yet Richard was unmistakably different. He was 16 years old and dying. Despite that reality, he was almost magical in the love he constantly poured out to his mother, his brother, and to those who cared for him. The "Richard is Amazing" stories overflowed.

As amazing as he was, Richard worried a lot. He worried not about himself, but about those around him. When he did not go to school because he was really sick or was forced to use oxygen, he worried about Bob, his friend and hired male aide at school. Bob was one of the individuals with whom Richard talked most about his illness in a fraternity of male bonding.

"He is very fond of Bob," Richard's mom said. "When he didn't go to school this week, Richard was worried for Bob—that Bob would be out of a job, because he didn't have anything to do. I tell him, don't worry about Bob. They'll find something for him to do," his mom added.

Humor often becomes a key coping mechanism during end-of-life times. Such was the case for Richard and his community. Although talking at times was difficult given his breathing issues, he never failed to tell his hospice care workers that they could only come back to his house and see him when they had first stopped by Toys-R-Us on the way.

His mom told the story of when Richard first had his G-tube inserted for eating. "He was in the hospital. His cousins came over to see him, and he said: 'Watch. I'm going to show you a trick. Look, I'm eating: no hands!'"

Not only did Richard make fun of his own physical situation, he made fun of how society collectively talks about the plight of those like him who are dying. Richard quite often used the word "death" in talking about himself and his situation. What he also enjoyed talking about even more were all the words or phrases people use in place of the death word. His list was priceless, and his smile unending as he shared each one:

Kick the bucket
Buy the farm
Cross the river

Pushing up daisies
Taking a dirt nap

Even the hospice workers delighted in picking up on Richard's rhetorical cue. It was as if Richard set the tone and the verbal cues for talking about his situation. Without a doubt, he was comfortable with the word death, and he never seemed to deny the reality of his situation.

Within their family structure, Richard, his mom, and his little brother, Alonzo, spent a great deal of time and energy protecting each other. Alonzo was born perfectly healthy in 1998 and is 11 years old.

Richard and Alonzo, who looked much the same, acted like typical brothers. They wrestled and boxed together, played jokes on one another, got on each other's nerves, and most of all *protected* one another. When the family was sent a new hospice nurse, Richard and his mom told the nurse she need not be offended when Alonzo tried to take over the situation to protect and help Richard.

"I said, please don't get offended. I said that sometimes, like when I was coughing, and the new nurse was saying, 'do you need your bucket to cough into,' well, Alonzo, he thinks that's his job. He'll go and get it. When mechanical alarms go off (signaling Richard is in physical trouble), and Alonzo goes and . . . says: 'That's my job, that's my job to take care of my big brother!' "

Tireless hospice workers caring for Richard love to tell about Alonzo's parting words and rituals every evening when they finished taking care of his brother: "Thank you for taking care of my brother!" Alonzo would say to them. After walking them out of the modest mobile home with the long wheelchair ramp,

Alonzo checked under their cars for strange things, or scanned their cars with flashlights to make sure all was well for the evening. The hospice workers would thank him.

Alonzo then asked them to beep their car horns at him so that he would know they were safe as they drove away. The same words were said and the same actions taken almost every evening.

The noise of car horns beeping brought simple comfort and solace to a very grown-up 11-year-old boy named Alonzo, a boy who loved his dying brother.

Richard also worked hard to try to protect his mother from sadness and crying; no easy task, she admitted.

"He doesn't like for me to cry for anything," Richard's mom commented.

Richard replied, "She cries at everything. You big baby!" Richard then flashed his huge smile and gazed affectionately at his mom, who did not disagree with the assessment. She readily admitted the tears flow easily and always have. She used much the same self-effacing humor as her son in responding: "I cried the first day of school. I cry the last day of school. I cry when he goes into another pant size." She laughed. She described her oldest son as being her protector, "my man of the house."

Richard was extremely close to his grandfather. "I love my grandpa," Richard commented. It was Richard's grandfather who would always hold him tight when Richard was feeling as if he were going to die.

During these times, Richard's grandfather would always console him and say, "When the time comes, who's going to be waiting for you on the other side? Remember? Who's going to be waiting there for you?"

"Grandma," Richard would reply.

One of Richard's ultimate goals was not just to have a 16th birthday party at Hooter's, but also to have a high school graduation party. His goal was to graduate with his class of 2006. He told his mom, "You know, Mom, instead of a birthday party, I want a graduation party. Oh, wow!"

And yet Richard never made his goal of graduating in 2006. He died in late November of 2003, in the early morning hours of a Thanksgiving weekend.

Perhaps for Richard there was a notion of Fight or Freedom, as compared to the proverbial notion of Fight or Flight. Although his body failed to let him reach his high school graduation goal, in no way did Richard run away from death. In fact, he embraced his dying in the same way he embraced living. He talked about it with grace and humor far beyond his 16 years of age. Richard's long-time school mentor, a gentleman far older than him, said as a part of his eulogy: "I did not mentor Richard. Richard mentored me."

Physical freedom now abounds for Richard. No longer does he have to be tethered to or embarrassed by oxygen. No longer does he have to cough into a bucket. Perhaps life on the other side, in whatever shape or form that may take, represents the final and truest form of freedom for Richard. His mother believes so.

Before he died, Richard asked Dr. Johnson about her notion of heaven. He explained to her that he wasn't worried about dying, but he was concerned about missing all of his favorite television shows. Dr. Johnson reassured Richard that televisions were on 24 hours a day in heaven, and he could watch anything he wanted, anytime.

Epilogue

The "Hooters guy," who embraced life and taught so many others how to do the same in the process, died quietly in his own bed, with his mother sleeping on the floor next to his side. On the evening of his death, he seemed to feel much better than earlier in the week. He wanted to watch a movie, and he said very clearly, "I need a candy bar."

He spent time with his beloved grandfather, mother, and little brother. He was unusually and especially concerned with being clean. He wanted to make sure his fingernails were all clean and his face perfectly clean-shaven. He asked his grandfather to hand shave him, even after being shaved using an electric razor. This was unusual behavior. His mom said it was as if he was preparing for a new life in which he wanted to make a good first impression.

When his mom awoke on her own accord in the middle of the morning, she immediately knew Richard was not breathing. For some reason he did not have any coughing fits right before his death, unlike so many times before. His eyes were closed, and his mouth was no longer open as if fighting for his last breaths. His mom kissed him and said at least now he would never have to wear oxygen again.

During the funeral visitation time, Richard's treasured protector brother, Alonzo, worked the crowd in his crisp white button-down shirt, black creased pants, and shiny patent shoes. Every few minutes Alonzo would glance at his mother, as if to make sure she was still standing. Then he would return to the open casket and touch the hand of his champion and departed brother, clothed in a blue high school sports jersey. Richard would have been, or was, proud.

⚜

Perhaps the night of his death Richard knew what was going to happen. Maybe an unusual cleaning ritual became one way for Richard to prepare for what was to come. Maybe he wanted to look his very best to see others. Whatever the reason, being clean and extra-handsome on this one particular night seemed of critical importance.

In the words and beliefs of his grandfather, Richard most assuredly was going to see his grandmother again, his guardian angel. She would reach down, give him a big hug and kiss, and say hi. The "Hooters Guy" had indeed graduated.

The Hooters Guy
An Interviewer's Perspective

A Lesson Learned - *Dreaming*

Hooters Restaurant is a national chain of restaurants catering to men. It proudly displays a picture of three well-endowed beautiful women on its Internet home page. The chest areas of the women are covered with the tag line: Delightfully Tacky Yet Unrefined. The lead news story from the Hooters' home page is designed to solicit votes for a waitress in the running for the 2008 Playmate of the Year.

So picture this: in comes a young boy in a wheelchair using oxygen, with his mom and nurses and hospice chaplain by his side. While he may be there to eat a hamburger, his bigger mission is to celebrate his 16th birthday – and most likely his last – by *dreaming*.

All of the young people I interviewed had dreams they were trying hard to fulfill. Some of those dreams took them to fun and unusual places like Hooters Restaurant for just a few hours one afternoon. Some of the dreams took whole families to exotic places across the country for weeks at a time.

Whether healthy, wrestling with life-threatening illnesses, caring for others, or dying ourselves, let us never give up on dreaming. The Hooters Guy would want nothing less.

Suggested Response Strategies/Discussion Questions/ Commentary:

** Think about the following questions:
    —Knowing that everyone dies eventually, what are your dreams before you die? How are you going to

make them come true? What is standing in your way, and how can you remove or change it?

—What are the dreams of those you love, including and most especially someone close to you who may be dying? How can you help make those dreams come true?

—If upon the deaths of loved ones there are lost dreams, how will you grieve for those losses?

—Are there ways you can make the lost dreams come alive in new and different ways?

—Are there ways you can make the dreams of those who have died live on long after their deaths?

** Start a *dream journal* where you write down or draw pictures or create symbols of your own dreams, along with a possible timeline and strategy plan for carrying them out.

** Talk out loud about your dreams and/or the dreams of those whom you love and who may be dying. Surround yourself with people who will help you make your dreams come true, as opposed to others who may make fun of your dreams or diminish them in any way.

** Give yourself permission to let go of lost dreams or dreams that just will not happen in this lifetime.

** Let your dreams take you into unusual or different places, just like The Hooters Guy did with his own dreams.

Your Personal Notes/Action Steps:

-3-

INTELLECTUAL CAPITAL

In a capital city of a large state, a very smart and loving family rests a little easier now that son, Marcus, age five, is in remission from a rare and potentially deadly form of leukemia. The cancer struck Marcus when he was 24 months old. Marcus' mom, Kandace, knew something was wrong.

"Marcus had been sick. He had been on antibiotics. We thought that he had an ear infection," she stated in a matter-of-fact manner. "He was only 24 months old and could not verbalize a lot. But you know, he just didn't look good."

Kandace was the first to wonder if Marcus had leukemia. She continued to be concerned about his overall appearance and his inability to come back from the ear infection, or what could possibly have been the flu.

"I had actually gotten online, wondering what could this be and had come across, you know, it's funny, because most kids, if they don't have the measles, mumps, flu, the basic stuff, then it goes immediately to the really ugly stuff. You know, like cancer," she explained.

Kandace searched the web in detail. On one particular search engine, called Web MD, she entered Marcus' specific symptoms. The word leukemia appeared.

"I had a doctor's appointment for him to go back to the pediatrician, but the night before, I went to a book store and saw a book on leukemia. I picked it up and just looked at the symptoms and freaked out," Kandace explained. The book presented the symptoms of leukemia in greater detail, including joint pain that can manifest itself in preventing children from wanting to walk. That was Marcus. "That really triggered fear in my mind," she said.

The next afternoon was Marcus' appointment with a local pediatrician. Early that morning, Kandace called the pediatrician and asked if they could come in now. That morning the pediatrician told Kandace he did not think Marcus had leukemia, but he would do the blood test just to make certain.

"He had this little machine in his office. Then he said this is definitely some kind of leukemia," Kandace said. That was all the information he would give her at the time.

Kandace took Marcus straight to the pediatric hospital. His dad, John, met them there. Thus began the family's chaotic journey into the world of cancer. It began almost as fast as Kandace had searched Web MD and pulled up the word leukemia.

Marcus and his parents spent the first night at a local children's hospital trying to make arrangements for the future, or at least the next 24 hours, as they redefined *their* new future.

"We thought that it was bad, but more our take on it was, we need to find the best place in the world and get on a plane and go there," John said. The next day the family left for St. Jude Children's Research Hospital in Memphis, Tennessee.

Marcus' older sister, Debra, stayed behind with friends so that her fifth birthday party scheduled that day would not have to be cancelled.

"I went in my imagination," Debra remembered. Parents John and Kandace did remember to cancel the dinner party they were having that evening, but they forgot to notify everyone whom they had invited. While a few unaware dinner guests stood on a darkened front porch, the family was well on its way to St. Jude. Chaos on a variety of levels seems an initial part of most pediatric cancer diagnoses.

❧

For most families, hearing the initial diagnosis of an illness such as cancer for a child triggers the onslaught of a living nightmare. For some, the word is among the ugliest in the English language. Just as many remember that notable day in Dallas when President John F. Kennedy was assassinated, nearly all parents of children with advanced illnesses seem to remember the exact day and time when they were first told their children had life-threatening illnesses. Some parents wet their pants; some simply drop to the floor. Others have to have the message repeated, sometimes again and again.

In the case of Marcus' family, the physician handing them the initial diagnosis said the word leukemia in such a low tone in an attempt to be soothing that the family initially missed the diagnosis.

"I remember the physician was very soft spoken. We couldn't hear him. I probably had a wiggling toddler on my lap and some chattering. I remember not hearing anything," Kandace said. She asked that he repeat what he had just said.

Many doctors say they struggle with the delivery of bad news. Physicians suggest that only in recent years has training been initiated in medical schools whereby physicians are taught how to work with the families of dying patients, as they wrestle with death themselves. Such was not the case in the early 1980s.

"Doctors were taught to distance themselves emotionally, and I think that's wrong," a pediatric pulmonary physician states. "You can't let it impair your judgment, but I no longer fight it," she says.[1]

Marcus' parents are well-educated individuals. Both have strong academic and professional credentials. Tackling Marcus' cancer from an intellectual capacity will always be a core strategy for the family. Included in that process is the way in which Marcus' physicians communicate with Kandace and John as they direct their son's care. They respectfully contrast their hunger for straightforward, smart, and the latest available detailed medical information with other families who may only want a "thumbs up/thumbs down" response. Plain talk, as John and Kandace call it, does not work with those families, but they recognize and appreciate everyone's diversity in the range of information desired.

"Something that I know the physicians struggle with, and it's a fine line, is not to overwhelm the parent. There is just so much information to be reported," Kandace said. "My brain was just trying to reach back to college biology, you know, when you are talking about white cells and platelets. It can be very technical, trying to understand it.

"When I encounter a new physician, I find myself kind of sending him or her cues, you know, that we are educated. There is so much to grasp. The physicians are trying hard to make this understandable—putting things in very simple terms. And we get frustrated with that because we both feel like we've earned honorary degrees," Kandace said.

In remembering the initial and subsequent conversations with the soft-spoken physician, Kandace said, "I remember sending cues to Dr. Jones. We told him, look, very straight out, we are both educated. Please don't talk down to us."

John and Kandace wanted messages that delivered two things: (1) options and (2) answers. Generalizations and platitudes became shrill violations against how they viewed themselves as young professionals and most especially as educated parents of a young child who had cancer. Making decisions based on personalities or trite sayings was not an option for them.

"I remember I was talking with Dr. Jones on the phone that day, telling him that we had made the decision to move Marcus from their hometown hospital to St. Jude in Tennessee. And I said, 'That's my advice from my sister who has the most medical training in my family. She's an oncology nurse, and I just have to trust that.' And his response was, 'I wish you would trust me.' I was just like—I so don't need this right now."

Once the family arrived at St. Jude, they were given many options, answers, and very detailed information as to how specific medical protocols would be used on Marcus. Upon the family's initial arrival, the front-line medical staff spent at least ten minutes simply explaining the features of the room in which Marcus had been placed, long before conversations began about his treatment plans.

Even when the conversations did not represent options or answers for the family, somehow the St. Jude staff managed to deliver the messages in such a way so as to avoid the gross generalizations and small talk that had initially frustrated the parents. Both Kandace and John attributed the change in communication style at St. Jude to a focus on research as opposed to practice.

"The doctor came in the first night we arrived at St. Jude. He was a resident. Not even a leukemia guy; he's a solid tumor guy," Kandace explained. "He took a lot of information. That was part of what he was doing. But he also explained so much. And he wasn't hurried; he was just there. I think we probably spent about two hours with him...."

John quickly interjected, "which was funny because the gist of what he really had to tell us was: we are not going to do anything until Monday morning. I think it had to do with the difference of a human being and a focus on practice versus research. These are people at St. Jude that actually do spend all their time, when they are not treating patients, thinking about better ways to treat patients, better ways to fight the disease."

Marcus spent many months at St. Jude. At the time of the interview, he and his parents continued to travel back and forth for follow-up treatments. He also continues to see physicians in his hometown.

When asked how the parents communicated with two-year-old Marcus during this process, both Kandace and John acknowledged doing "weird" things to both continually entertain and distract Marcus. Finding word substitutions became an important part of that language of weirdness.

For example, Marcus has always loved choo-choo trains. The pajamas he was wearing on the day of his interview, which he proudly showed to everyone in the room, were covered in colorful trains. He likes to make the sound of trains.

Thus, when Marcus first began treatment at age two, the port that was surgically placed into his body for delivering his chemotherapy became his choo-choo. The dressing placed on top of the port became the train station or the route; the little pillow that holds up the port became the platform.

As he grew older, Marcus began to send the family cues that he knew what was going on with his body. He began to understand what the actual medical words meant and what certain treatments would entail.

"And then one time," Kandace recalled, "you know in front of Marcus we would always call the port 'choo-choo,' and then we would talk to the nurses about the port." Finally Marcus turned to his mother out of the clear blue sky and said, "that's not my choo-choo, that's my port!" Marcus was approximately three at the time.

Marcus also quickly picked up a lot of the medical terminology beyond the word *port*. When the time came for Marcus to receive shots or take medicines, Kandace would usually say to her husband in front of Marcus, "I think it's time to administer his pharmaceuticals," a way to say medicine without him running away. Yet she explained that even as early as age three, Marcus knew what was coming when he heard the phrase "administer his pharmaceuticals."

"He knew. He caught on very quickly," Kandace said.

Knowing the minute details associated with pediatric cancer and leukemia data is critically important to

Kandace and John. They view themselves as researchers who continually study and learn the many statistics associated with their son's disease.

Without looking at a sheet of paper, they succinctly told me that one in two million children is diagnosed each year with the same kind of leukemia Marcus has experienced.

Fortunately Marcus remains in remission to date. The parents were quick to correct me when I mistakenly refer to Marcus' disease in the present tense. They do not want Marcus described as a young person who has leukemia.

"Actually Marcus doesn't have leukemia. He's in remission. Well, he's still on treatment, so it's kind of a personal choice on words, ones that we think are important, and we certainly emphasize with him," Kandace explained as she corrected me. "He probably went into remission day seven of treatment, which most kids with leukemia do. But they still think that on a molecular level, he still might have leukemia, so they continue to treat him for about three years. But their clinical definition of remission most kids reach in the first month." The family remains ever vigilant in keeping up with the latest technology and information on the disease as their son continues to receive preventative treatment.

Despite being frequently frustrated with physicians who deliver messages in perceived simplistic or patronizing ways, both John and Kandace are grateful for the medical care and technology they have found both in Memphis and their hometown. It has kept Marcus alive so far.

This time in their lives is spent holding each other close, enjoying lazy Saturday mornings, reminiscing, looking at photographs of the many times Marcus has been in various hospitals, and reading the latest information on leukemia. Marcus and his eight-year-old sister, Debra, seem exceptionally close. They look out for and take care of each other.

People tell John and Kandace they are to be admired for their unending reliance on intellectual capital in responding to Marcus' cancer. They are told they come across as extremely poised and graceful in the way in which they have faced this chapter in their lives. They suggest otherwise:

Kandace:	It's not always that graceful.
John:	Graceful, nor pretty.
Kandace:	Stress brings out a lot of ugly.

Revisiting their son's initial diagnosis and the early days and months of Marcus' cancer is not something Kandace nor John care to do. However, they choose to do so in an effort to provide both education and reassurance to other parents in similar situations.

"I know there have been studies on what kind of information parents wish they had heard, and one thing that doctors don't tend to address that parents really want to hear: it's like the fourth most requested thing— *reassurance*," Kandace explained. "You need a lot of assurance that you caught this as soon as you possibly could have, that this wasn't neglect. Every parent I know completely beats themselves up over it. That's funny; it's really like a first stage thing. You really are caught up in *why*. Then it goes out the window. And you

don't think about why, ever again. That's the way it is,"
she declared.

Intellectual Capital
An Interviewer's Perspective

A Lesson Learned – *Studying*

Marcus' parents were doggedly determined to learn all they could about their son's disease in order to put up a strong fight on a collective front. Even before seeing a doctor for the first time—but knowing intuitively that something was very wrong—Marcus' mom was searching the web for information and scouring through bookstore shelves while thinking about Marcus' symptoms.

Studying reliable sources about the disease we ourselves or our loved ones are facing is critically important throughout the healthcare process as people change and diseases progress. With that said, however, we should also carefully scrutinize the source of the information we are receiving to make certain it is credible, accurate, and up to date given the ever-changing complexities of medical care and treatments.

Suggested Response Strategies/Discussion Questions/ Commentary:

** Buy or find a Care Notebook to write down notes from conversations with medical providers at the time they occur. While many medical caregivers may be stretched thin on time, ask your physicians to repeat the information they are giving you. First listen to what is being said; then write down that same information in note form in a way that makes sense to you. Ask your physicians, nurse practitioners, chemotherapy providers, and others to review the notes you have written for accuracy and completeness. Keep the Care Notebook up to date.

** Include in your Care Notebook places for you to file brochures, articles, reference lists, and other informative materials about the subject matters in which you or your loved ones are interested.

** Be thorough in your study efforts. Do not just read what is on the Internet; also visit libraries, contact resource organizations, and locate support groups in your area.

** Be diligent yet practical in your studying efforts. If you are facing times of serious illnesses for you or your loved ones, be realistic in what you can and cannot accomplish. Do the best you can, and never forget to ask for help. Now is not the time to be heroic – just studious and informed.

Your Personal Notes/Action Steps:

-4-

PRAISING LIFE

Shannon and David Ede and their children are individually and collectively one of the most beautiful families I have ever seen. Together they look much like an ensemble cast on a Hollywood movie screen. Mom Shannon looks like Nicole Kidman, complete with long, wavy red hair and porcelain skin. Dad David looks like Kevin Klein. Their three children, Patrick and his siblings, Daniel and Ellen, are equally beautiful with translucent smiles, complexions, and sparkling eyes. The family smiles and laughs a lot. They obviously enjoy being together.

Yet their world of physical beauty and happy times became an emotional nightmare on November 26, 2002, when 11-year-old Patrick was diagnosed with acute myeloid leukemia (AML).

The American Cancer Society and the National Cancer Institute identify leukemia as the most common form of cancer in children and adolescents. It accounts for nearly one-third of all cancers in children under the age of 15, and one-fourth of all cancers occurring before the age of 20.

Acute myeloid leukemia (AML) is a rare form of pediatric leukemia. It is a cancer of the blood-forming tissue usually found in the bone marrow and lymph nodes. The bone marrow of persons with leukemia begins producing large numbers of abnormal and immature blood cells that are usually white blood cells. These "bad" cells are oftentimes called blasts. Blasts flood the blood and lymph streams and then may invade vital organs such as the brain, testes, ovaries, or skin. In some rare cases, AML tumor cells may form solid tumors called isolated granulocytic sarcoma or chloroma.

Early signs of AML may include fever, chills, bleeding or bruising, swollen lymph nodes, and other symptoms that are flu-like such as weakness, chronic weariness, or aching bones and joints. In Patrick's case, two days before Thanksgiving in 2002, he went to his physician. He was in immediate pain.

"My bones had been hurting more. My arms and legs had really been hurting, and I couldn't sleep at night because it hurt so much. And I thought it was growing pains. So we went to the doctor and asked if we could see blood work. And later, he diagnosed me," Patrick calmly stated.

Parents use a variety of words and phrases to describe their reactions to hearing the news for the first time that one of their children has cancer. Some calmly rattle off long names of specific diseases. Others take a chronological, journal-like approach in telling you where they specifically went each day, who they saw, what they did, and what each physician, nurse, and others said at every point along the way. In some cases, the reactions are beyond words and descriptions.

"Just for the record, I mean, we all had moments," Shannon, Patrick's mom, said. "When I first heard Patrick's diagnosis, I had a visceral response. I actually felt like I might soil my pants, but I didn't."

Patrick's father, David, has also had his moments of despair and darkness. Shannon described a sentinel moment for her husband that occurred later on in their son's illness when the pain for Patrick was excruciatingly horrible.

"David laid out on the hospital floor one time in tears because Patrick was in pain, and the morphine wasn't touching his pain. The nurses weren't responding, and it was so frustrating." There is a sense in talking with this family that normally David seldom losses his composure.

Regardless of what came the family's way, the 11-year-old boy at the center of the storm seemed to rise above it all.

"I think Patrick is given a special grace because I have seen him respond more negatively emotionally to algebra before and since cancer than he did the whole cancer journey. I'm not kidding you. I think he was really given a special grace," Shannon said.

Shannon also talked about her son and his philosophy regarding his illness within a notion of control. She is proud that Patrick remains in control of his own decision making and life living to the extent humanly possible. Shannon suggests Patrick sees himself as being in control of his destiny: "not to get boring, he's just fairly in control, of thinking 'okay, this is my responsibility in setting this thing.'"

Another verbal exchange reaffirmed much the same sentiment. It also added a dimension held by the whole family: they were not alone in the journey.

Shannon: We explained to Patrick that he has cancer, but he was shockingly accepting right from the start.

Interviewer to Patrick: Any idea why?

Patrick: I knew that it was in God's hands.

When asking expectant parents when their babies are due, many of the responses are defined in terms of weeks, sometimes to the point of needing to conduct a mental mathematical exercise in order to understand the answer. When talking with parents of children with advanced disease about their experiences, such is not the normal experience. Time frames are much shorter and bound very tightly in terms of upcoming treatments and physician visits.

Weeks may seem like an eternity in the worlds of children and young people who have cancer. Minutes and hours seem to dictate a cancer family's calendar as they try to cope with what has now become a different type of long-term future.

The Ede family web site, www.caringbridge.org/tx/patrickede/, describes one particular day in the almost-daily postings of Patrick's progress in terms of hourly time limits:

December 5, 2002:   Patrick gets to go home for about 30 hours.

Upon the initial diagnosis, the family remembered that Patrick started on chemotherapy within a matter of hours. The simple difference in expectations from one hour or one day to the next can bring major highs or lows. Patrick and his parents also remembered an especially joyful time in which he ran ahead of schedule.

"It surprised us the day that he got out of isolation. This time, day 21 would be the earliest that he should ever come out. But he had recovered enough to where it was safe for him to come on out," Shannon said. "But Patrick, on day 14, his white cells rebounded, and he made a great recovery, so he was a week earlier on getting out of isolation. I was going to get my mask and gloves on, and he said, 'no mamma.' Then those tears just started coming, and he came in and hugged all of us, and we're all boo-hooing," she added.

One of the communication items mentioned repeatedly by the family is the Patrick Ede web site suggested by Patrick's Uncle Johnny. The web site is a part of the Caring Bridge (www.caringbridge.org) organization, a web site designed to help young people and their families stay in touch and be informed throughout their healthcare journeys. Shannon describes the web site and the communication available to her at her fingertips as the "birth of communication—it's just huge. Patrick can communicate with other people. So now it will allow us to rally support and can also tell us what we need. People right away started sending us e-mails and stuff, telling us jokes, and to try to reach him," she added.

Although he was too sick to look at it directly, Patrick enjoyed hearing about the web site because it allowed him to connect not only with his healthy friends, but also other cancer patients and seriously ill kids who made him smile. When asked if he personally looked at the e-mails, he responds: "Yeah, a whole bunch. There are little six year olds, you know, saying, now I've got a joke that I would like to tell," Patrick said.

Shannon viewed the web site as catharsis both for her husband, David, and Patrick.

"David would sit down there and daily see what's going on. It was more than just a lot of medical facts. There were some spiritual things that we were learning, or things that we all needed. So it was really a helpful thing. It was nice for me to not have to carry that, because with any burden I get impatient. For now, David could just do that, and it took some of the stress off Patrick, too," Shannon said.

Patrick's parents perceived a variety of benefits from the web site. Shannon suggested that the web represents a method for people all over the world to write to the family, and "at our leisure, we could read through them. People would write, and they would send unbelievable prayers and jokes and stories and so that way, it was a no-hassle way of communicating effectively. Like we could look at that if we wanted to, or we didn't have to," she added.

The family also believes this new birth in communication is a way for patients such as Patrick to avoid becoming isolated in an environment where sometimes direct contact can be costly, if not deadly.

"When Patrick was really so sick, he did not get out and interact with the kids at the children's hospital here," Shannon says. "He's kind of introverted. He never felt well enough to get out there. We did see this one boy who was the same age who was out there yukin' it up with the nurses. We were going, 'what, are you really sick?' In the MDA (MD Anderson Cancer Center), he had never really felt well enough to go and make friends with the kids, but there you are in isolation where you are not allowed to be outside. It was like he got peer support from the web site because it was easier to write to people that way," Shannon stated.

David also believed the web site, which contains daily updates on Patrick's condition as well as his whereabouts in terms of being at the hospital or at home, represented a much-preferred method of communication for families like his.

"It's so much better than e-mail because e-mail is sort of a *push* type of communication: here I'm pushing this to you. But the web site was more *pull*. It was basically: here it is if you are interested. So, it wasn't very intrusive communication," David added.

The web site also became a way to ask for help and to sort through emotions throughout the hospital vigils. The family routinely asked for people to rally on Patrick's behalf with prayers when times became really tough. David also used the routine of connecting with the web site as a form of sense making.

"That was actually an exercise in discipline for me to have to sit down at the end of the day and do all the events, all my emotions, all my thoughts," David said. "It sort of made sense. So that was real good for me. Also, people want to know what is happening, moment by moment."

Real-life activities of daily living remind us that conversing with children and young people in the best of times is frequently challenging. Thus when children like Patrick are thrust into a foreign and frightening world like the world of cancer, parents oftentimes search for new and simplistic ways to explain harsh and complicated scientific realities to their children. In Patrick's case, nonverbal communication became an increasingly important way of understanding what was happening, and what was to yet come.

"We were trying to get him ready for Houston (MD Anderson). First of all, we were trying to give him a scope for a different environment," Shannon said. "I showed him three fingers, and that was three different phases that we were going through."

The three-finger roller coaster: Both Shannon and David used the three-finger method throughout the journey to help Patrick gauge where he was in his treatment plan, and what was awaiting him around the corner. The three-finger method became an explanatory tool for helping Patrick understand the initial phases of his treatment, which included induction therapy, in which chemotherapy is used to try to kill as many of the leukemia cells as possible so that the disease will go into remission. Then the second and third phases, intensification and consolidation therapy, are designed to kill any remaining leukemia cells once the leukemia is in remission.

The three-finger method became a calendar for the family in terms of holiday and major events. Because Patrick was first diagnosed during Thanksgiving week, treatments were being given in the midst of the Thanksgiving and Christmas seasons. Shannon would anticipate Patrick's questions, such as, "Where is Christmas going to be?"

"Christmas is going to be right around here. You will still be in the hospital, just so you kind of know," his mother replied. Throughout the conversation, she again referenced a certain number of fingers along with specific points along her fingers and the areas in between. Shannon's nonverbal, picturesque method of communicating using this three-finger method almost seemed to parody a roller coaster ride, with higher moments at the tops of the tracks, followed by the inevitable extreme dips or lows that were just ahead of the curves in each stage of the treatment.

"I would say: 'So, Patrick, here is where we are right now. We're this far, and you still have this far you need to go.' We kind of always had a scope ahead of him," she explained.

One of the higher moments of the journey that eventually led to Patrick's remission came in the form of a bone marrow transplant (BMT). According to the National Cancer Institute, bone marrow transplantation is a newer type of treatment against AML in which a patient's bone marrow is replaced with healthy bone marrow from another person whose tissue is the same as or almost the same as the patient's. Bone marrow transplantation takes place once high doses of chemotherapy are given to the patient in order to destroy all of the bone marrow in the diseased body.

Again the family turned to the web to make an appeal for individuals to come forward so that they might be tested for possible matches with Patrick. On December 14, 2002, over 150 people came forward to be tested. Within that group, one individual wanted desperately to help Patrick: his little brother, Daniel. As Shannon explained, "All Daniel wanted to do was be the donor, that's *all* he wanted to do."

On December 17, 2002, less than one month after Patrick's first diagnosis, younger brother Daniel found out he would get his Christmas wish: to be a bone marrow donor for his brother. When Daniel first heard the news, his mom said the reddish-haired exuberant boy went running through the house, jumping up and down, and shouting over and over at the top of his lungs: "It's me!!! It's me!!! It's me!!!"

On March 11, 2003, Daniel underwent a bone marrow aspiration at 2:30 P.M. in which bone marrow was taken from his body in one part of MD Anderson, while Patrick waited in another. The boys' parents said the first words out of Daniel's mouth after the procedure were: "Did I help my brother?" "Then," Shannon laughed and said, "he just blows chow (throws up) all over the place, you know, because he's feeling awful."

Again nonverbal communication became important to the family.

"They let Daniel out of his procedure. We went straight up to see Patrick, let him know that his bone marrow was coming," Shannon explained. "There wasn't a lot of fanfare from the doctors in terms of Daniel donating his bone marrow. I was walking through while the doctors were finishing their paperwork, and the nurses were over there. I was like, 'hey, let's give it up for the donor!' I made everybody applaud," she said.

Patrick received Daniel's bone marrow beginning at 6:20 P.M. that same day. Twelve days later, his blood counts improved to the point that he could be removed from "isolation." On March 25, 2003, Patrick was released from MD Anderson.

As of this writing, Patrick remains at home in remission. His head is now full of beautiful dark hair. He no longer looks like Gollum from *The Lord of the Rings* trilogy, as another young boy called him after he went bald from receiving massive amounts of chemotherapy. If it were not for the white surgical mask that Patrick occasionally wears in public, one might never know of his ordeal or that he has had any experiences different from any other healthy young boy.

❦

The family posted the following update on their web site at 8:47 P.M., CST, on Wednesday, October 29, 2003:

Patrick is doing really well. We're back from two weeks in California and we had a great time, thanks to the Make-a-Wish Foundation (www. wish.org). We arrived in Burbank on October 11, spent several days in Ventura with Shannon's brother, then rented a 25-foot motor home and drove up the coast along Highway 1 north. We camped along the way at Morro Bay, Big Sur River, then Carmel for 2 nights and then landed in Yosemite where we stayed 5 days. It was absolutely gorgeous. We were all in awe of the beauty of God's creation and could not stop looking up at the tall trees and huge mountains all around. The weather was perfect. We slept about 10 hours per night. We could not have asked for more. . . . Patrick continues to do well. He has not had any serious illness since being released from MD Anderson 7 months ago! One reason that we chose to rent an RV and go camping was because we wanted to avoid large crowds and too many public places, due to Patrick's immune suppression. Although all his clinic visits and lab tests have been positive, he is only seven months past his bone marrow transplant, and he is still at risk for illness, infection, and relapse.

Both Patrick's parents talk about a variety of responses that they have seen from other parents who are also making their ways through the horror of having children with cancer. They talk about "fear and paralysis, anger (why me?) or God help us."

Through their own emotional roller coasters, they have and continue to experience both anger and an intense desire to run and hide. Shannon remembers the

time when the family went by the MD Anderson chapel
to pray. A statue of an angel was in the room, and below
it the saying was "Fear Not."

Shannon recalls: "And so my heart is going boom,
boom, boom. I'm terrified at this point. It wasn't a home-
like setting, where everything is totally different. And
God, you know how your first encounter with something is usually the right way and everything else seems
to be wrong? Even though we know that, we were like
'do this right, do this right.' We were kind of irritated. I
see this *fear not,* and I'm about to come unglued, and I
think it's okay to fall apart. I said to Patrick, 'don't be
scared. It says *fear not.*' But he was fine," she adds.

Patrick has sustained his family throughout this
trauma, and they have sustained him. The family holds
tight to each other, physically and emotionally, and
continues to work hard to keep focused on the situation
at hand, as they did when Patrick was in the three
phases of his treatment. They refuse to continually hide.
Even when they do, they know that "God will hear us,"
David says.

"There are a number of emotional features that
helped me, gave me focus and direction, and helped me
make sense," David said.... "And one of them was, you
know, on a daily basis, we would talk to a doctor and get
certain numbers of certain statistics. Well, you know,
our latest test shows this and that means this, and there
is this percent chance that this might happen. These
numbers are important."

Data became an increasingly important component
for the family's ability to remain focused on the eye of
whatever storm was coming their way. Data also became

an ongoing mechanism for a more spiritual under-standing of the family's definition of truth.

Patrick's dad uses a Biblical illustration to convey his family's notion of real truth. It's the story of Peter's challenge of Jesus to prove his identity by walking on water. David gives an overview of the story:

> "The disciples were on a boat in a big storm. And they were scared, and they said, what is that, Jesus' ghost? And he said no, it's ours. And Peter said, okay, if it's really you, then you step out of the boat. Peter walks out and, do you remember the story, he's doing okay. Then, the Bible says he starts to see the waves, and he takes his eyes off his goal. He starts to look at that stuff that gets in his way. And when this happens, he starts to sink."

David continues with the analogy by explaining that once when someone asked him how he copes with his family's situation, he responded, "We have all these facts and all this junk, all this medical junk. You can't focus; then you sink. It's not that you don't consider it, you don't ignore it. The question is: What are your eyes going to focus on? So Peter had a choice, and he made the wrong choice. So we had a choice, too. Now, are we going to look at the facts? These are medical facts, they are statistics, but they are not the truth. The truth for us is that God loves us, and that He is always with us, no matter what happens to us," David said.

Shannon is quick to add that for her family, spiritu-ality is not like a bandage or a pat on the back. "It was what your next breath was based on," she stated. She is also fully aware that sometimes there is a different outcome.

"We saw some other reality checks. MD Anderson lost 31 kids. In these next three months, things can change on the turn of a dime. So the reality is out there. We were just thankful that Patrick is still here, and we get to do these new things," Shannon added. In the midst of whatever new things come their way, the family will continue to rely on the help and grace of others, which has sustained them thus far.

Following Patrick's release from MD Anderson, the Ede family stood center stage on July 27th in a praise celebration at their church in front of approximately 250 friends and family who came to celebrate Patrick's remission and homecoming. These were individuals who had literally circled the family's Round Rock home in a prayer vigil. They were men and women who had donated blood. They were folks who had offered to give up some of their bone marrow so that Patrick could live. They had mowed the family's lawn, cleaned their home repeatedly, home-schooled Patrick's siblings, and delivered casseroles on top of casseroles. They had prayed and acted without ceasing. They were valiant heroes to these five individuals.

Shannon and David spoke to the crowd, at times crying and at other times talking in a clear united voice, firm and full with gratitude. They named individuals by name and by deed. They thanked groups of people. They thanked pastors and friends who were available both in Austin and Houston during hospital vigils.

For Shannon and David, and countless other families in which a child has a life-threatening illness, reliance on the outstretched hands of others may seem at first to be a sign of weakness or at a minimum, unfamiliarity. Soon enough, it becomes a matter of necessity and survival. As the family posts on their web: "We continue to find reasons to praise God, and that includes each of you." As the family tearfully hugged each other before the auditorium crowd, Patrick simply said quietly into the microphone: "Thank you all."

Data from the American Cancer Society show a five-year survival rate at approximately 40 percent for children with AML like Patrick. Advances in treatment continue to improve the odds, as will hopefully be the case for Patrick so that he may live well beyond his 12 years of age. For now, the family celebrates chronologically small, yet significant, victories like nine plus months of remission for Patrick.

David and Shannon fully understand the connection between data and the truth. They know now is a critical time.

"Although all his clinic visits and lab tests have been positive, Patrick is only seven months past his bone marrow transplant, and he is still at risk for illness, infection, and relapse. Although for the next four or five months, we will be going to MD Anderson only every three or four weeks, this is a critical time. One of Patrick's physicians told us that patients who relapse within the first year usually do so at the very end of their first year period. This may be due to the fact that any residual chemotherapy drugs have been eliminated from the patient's body toward the end of the first year, which may allow any remaining leukemia to reformulate," they wrote on their web site.

Yet that is not the final chapter for the Ede family, regardless of the data, or the odds, or the possibility of a relapse for Patrick. The final chapter for this family is one that is yet to come, in their minds. It represents the real truth of life for them: *God saves you.*

Patrick knows that God will save him in some form or fashion, even if it means departing this earth following a relapse. He and his family wholeheartedly believe their individual and collective final chapters are yet to come and will bear little resemblance to life known now. In the meantime, Patrick and his family are grateful for the present as they reflect on their web site:

> Again, this is a great reminder that there arc no guarantees regarding our future on this planet, and that applies to all of us. Although we know our ultimate destination, we do not know how or when we will be ushered from this life to the next, or how much pleasure we will enjoy or suffering we will endure until that time. We are grateful for today, and grateful for the guarantee of life eternal in heaven.

❧

The Patrick Ede Web site
www.caringbridge.org/tx/patrickede

Praising Life
An Interviewer's Perspective

Lesson Learned – *Celebrating*

Celebrating life. Patrick's brother, Daniel, shows so vividly a reality that we sometimes forget: most people truly want to help. Dealing with times of seriously-ill hardships and uncertainties is hard enough. There's no reason to go it alone. Celebrate those who want to help. And more importantly: *let them in.*

Suggested Response Strategies/Discussion Questions/ Commentary:

** When times are extremely tough, think about the many people who are helping you. Celebrate them. Give thanks in your own ways for their willingness to help.

** Celebrate milestones or important happenings of any kind and size: one step forward taken; ending chemotherapy; less pain; remission; financial assistance; going home.

** Use anniversary or milestone times to call and say thanks to others for their help, even if that help occurred months or years prior A celebration or thanksgiving call is never too late.

** Never forget to celebrate and care for yourself throughout the journey.

** Consider keeping a list of all of the guardian angels who are entering your life at this special time. If sending individual thank-you notes seems overwhelming and is just not going to happen, perhaps make a donation to a charitable organization like a hospice group on behalf of your helping group, or mention the group as a whole in a newsletter or church bulletin or some appropriate communication.

** Think about using the web, as the Ede family did, in letting people know how you or your loved one is doing. Celebrate the high points. Recognize the low points for what they are, yet knowing that something good can be found in every low point, however small or challenging to find.

Your Personal Notes/Action Steps:

-5-

LEONZO'S LEAD

Leonzo is 13 years old. For more than half of his life, he has wrestled with cancer. He was six when initially handed the diagnosis of leukemia.

Leonzo's specific form of leukemia is called acute lymphocytic leukemia (ALL). The American Cancer Society predicted in 2003 about 2,200 children in the United States would be diagnosed with ALL. Because of the advances being made in treatment over time, the five-year-survival rate for ALL patients is now nearly 80 percent.

Despite his young age, Leonzo wears many hats and juggles many balls in his battle with cancer. He is a first-generation English speaker. His mom speaks only Spanish. Throughout the years of his illness, Leonzo has grown into the roles of leader of his own basic health care, including serving as message deliverer and translator for his mom, given that most of his medical staff members do not speak Spanish.

People all around Leonzo seem to rely heavily on him. For a young boy who does not care to talk very much, he is placed most often at center stage, at least as observed on this particular afternoon. Part of the reason is functionality, given the language challenges between Leonzo's mom and the medical staff. Another reason is because Leonzo seems to be a take-charge, albeit quiet, leader of his own destiny.

At age six, Leonzo had a sense that something was physically wrong with him, but no one initially said anything directly to him. When asked how he knew something was amiss, he replies, "Because I looked at my mom, and she was sad." When I respond to that statement using the Spanish word *triste* for sad, Leonzo's mom, who is sitting quietly nearby, says faintly, "*sí, triste.*"

Perhaps she is referring to sadness then and now, and all the years in between that Leonzo has battled cancer. On this particular day, the sky is gray and gloomy, and Leonzo has just completed another week in a pediatric palliative care hospital—his home away from home. He hopes to leave the hospital that night. He will most likely return again.

Leonzo is the first to tell you that he has leukemia. He understands the importance of blood cultures and numbers and the worry that comes with the onset of a slight fever, like this one that has put him back in the hospital. However, things have changed over time in that Leonzo was not always told what was happening with his body, especially when he was much younger.

Initially, several days passed before Leonzo was told he was sick, even though he already knew something was wrong. Although he was only six at the time, he distinctly remembers the first time he officially learned he had leukemia.

Interviewer: "So, a few days passed (when he noticed his mom being sad), and your mom came in and said...?"

Leonzo: (He finishes the question): "She told me I had leukemia. And I took it as just a word."

Interviewer: "Just a word? Did you know what that meant?"

Leonzo: "No."

Interviewer: "What did you think?"

Leonzo: "Nothing."

Interviewer: "Did you ask her what it meant to you?"

Leonzo: "No."

Even though he asked little at the time, Leonzo seems to remember a great deal. He remembers not talking about his illness at the onset. He recalls closely watching his mom for a cue as to how things were going with him. He remembers, although somewhat vaguely, talking at times to his primary physician, Dr. Pete, whom he calls "a nice guy." "He's been nice to me," Leonzo says. His physician seems to be one of the few persons with whom Leonzo talks about his illness, even to this day.

Talking in general is not something Leonzo likes to do. He answers questions in brief form, usually with a yes or no answer, although he is extremely polite in conversing. Despite his brevity, however, he seems genuinely interested in and willing to tell his story, perhaps for no other reason than his beloved Dr. Pete asked him to do so.

"Do you ever like to talk about your illness?" I ask.

"No. I don't talk that much," he replies.

Leonzo has both older and younger siblings. They visit him in the hospital, where "we just play," he explains. They like to tell jokes and most of all, play Nintendo. Sometimes Leonzo wins. Sometimes he loses.

Leonzo and his siblings prefer game playing and joke telling in lieu of direct conversation. Outside the sibling circle, Leonzo sometimes uses humor about his own illness as a way to find new friends.

"If I didn't have this illness, I couldn't meet more persons," he states, explaining that his illness presents a way for him to meet new people. "At least, I think, a few of them," he added. He avoided going into greater detail on his thoughts in these areas, despite probing on my part.

Sometimes Leonzo likes to hear stories. Yet most of the time he prefers avoiding such conversation. "It brings memories," he says quietly, looking *triste,* much like his mother.

Leonzo sits in his home away from home, one of the rooms at the pediatric hospital. He spends a lot of the time looking out the window of what he calls his "second living room." He also likes to draw cars and flowers and dragons and tigers.

Much of his time is spent keeping up to date with his healthcare status. He listens closely to the numbers being given to him by the physicians and nurses about blood counts, body temperatures, cell levels, culture results, and on and on. He is told by people who are moving in and out quickly that certain treatments will happen for that particular day, provided previous tests turn out the way they are expected. Intravenous (IV) fluids and antibiotics are hung, and then taken down when the beeper goes off. New bags are hung. Everything happens almost automatically, yet the talk is often tough.

Leonzo seemed to be like many other young cancer patients in that he wants to hear straight talk about his condition. And that is exactly what he is given: straight talk from the hospital staff.

Staff Nurse: "I talk to Leonzo like he's my son. I tell him, and I'd be honest with him, I'd tell him: you need to take this medicine. This medicine sucks, it tastes nasty, but you are going to have to take it. You know that. And that's it. Don't I?" (The nurse looks at Leonzo, and Leonzo nods).

"And then when he doesn't get up in the morning I would take him my little normal saline and start dripping it on his head. Then he wakes up. Don't I?" The nurse again looks at Leonzo, who says, "yeah."

"I tell him he's going to eat his breakfast. If he doesn't, I'm going to eat it. His mama always brings him food. I don't know why we even have meals for him. Huevos and potatoes and his mom brings him tacos with hot sauce," the nurse says.

The tough talk from the nurse continues in front of Leonzo:

Staff Nurse:(Looking at Leonzo) "You know you have leukemia. That took over the transplant. There is nothing more we can do. When the leukemia takes over, you are going to go to heaven. And only God is going to decide when you go to heaven. When is that going to happen to you? Maybe in three months, maybe three years, maybe thirty years. It's when you get sick, you could die. So that is why we have to give you these drugs, these antibiotics, to keep you from getting sicker. . . . I know you have ALL (a serious form of leukemia), and I know you are going to die. But I don't care. I'm going to spend the time that I have with you having fun."

Leonzo wonders about the future. He prefers to think of himself now and in his future as a "normal" rather than a "sick" person. At times throughout the conversation, he seems more willing to think ahead. At other points, he becomes quite reticent.

Someday Leonzo hopes to become a physician. When asked what kind of physician he wants to be, he replies, "Like Dr. Pete." Dr. Pete is the tireless head of the hospital where Leonzo spends much of his time. He has taken care of Leonzo for the past seven years. Dr. Pete seems to be Leonzo's closest confidant. He is certainly his role model.

Leonzo's reticence about the future seems to stem from one kernel of truth: things are uncertain. What the future holds for Leonzo is highly ambiguous. He holds his cards close to his chest in the form of brief answers and few explanations. The uncertainty is troublesome and at times sad for Leonzo. It continues to make his mom *triste*. She is turning to the Bible for help and understanding.

Leonzo says hearing the staff talk about his dying makes him sad at times, but it does not worry him. He still sleeps well at night. He may draw dragons and tigers, but he does not seem to dream about them.

As his staff nurse says, Leonzo could live for three more months or maybe thirty years, although the latter is unlikely given the ALL disease itself and his present condition of fever spikes and frequent hospital visits. The hardest part is in the not knowing. Leonzo says he prefers not to talk to his mother or sisters or brothers at times because "sometimes they ask me questions I can't answer because I don't know it."

In the meantime, Leonzo will continue to lead the way on his own healthcare journey, regardless of its length. The staff believes he continues to have a good handle on his situation. As the afternoon of treatments and waiting draws to a close, a staff member speaks to the young boy, who has known sickness longer than not.

"Okay, I've got other patients, guy. So at 5 o'clock, in a few minutes, we will start our report, and I'm going to come back by and take some blood, and you will be discharged. A few minutes from now the doctor should be here, so I'm looking at a quarter of seven you should go home. So you will need to let your mama know," he told Leonzo. The directions to Leonzo continued to flow from the adult staff to the 13-year-old boy:

"There was some morphine, some boxes of morphine the pharmacy won't send up, so you will have to stop and get them on the way out. One of the healthcare nurses will come to your house to take care of you and give you more medicines. So let's say seven o'clock. It looks like you are already packed. Are you ready to go?"

As Leonzo nods affirmatively, he again looks around the room and glances at his mom who is eagerly awaiting the latest translation from her 13-year-old son. Leonzo has grown up fast. The scene represents an acute case of role reversal.

Before the interview closes, I ask Leonzo what others could learn from his experiences.

"If there were another leukemia patient in here who was just getting the diagnosis like you, what would you say to him or her?"

"Never give up," Leonzo replies with a smile.

Leonzo's Lead
An Interviewer's Perspective

A Lesson Learned – *Persevering*

Leonzo closed our interview with a simple yet profound statement: "never give up." *Persevering* is an important lesson to remember in progressing through times of chronic or terminal illnesses.

Perhaps for you the notion of persevering means that you continue to show up at the hospital or nursing home even when your loved one shows no signs of life or memory of who you are. Perhaps perseverance means insisting that your parents or older relatives for whom you are responsible (or yourself as well) get their affairs in order and make end-of-life care decisions while still healthy. For others perseverance may mean having hope upon receiving a bad diagnosis for the first time. For someone who is near death, persevering may mean hanging on until the last child or sibling arrives, and then letting go.

Whatever your journey, define your actions for yourself and set about persevering.

Suggested Response Strategies/Discussion Questions/ Commentary:

** Research has shown the value of writing in dealing with difficult times. Consider starting a personal and private journal of your situation, hopes, feelings, challenges, emotions, etc. as you persevere through the process.

Your Personal Notes/Action Steps:

-6-

AUTHENTICITY

At age 18, Eduardo is a wise sage who sits in the middle of his hospital bed, legs crossed, philosophizing about his life. Although he wishes he could live up north in the cold with the benefit of being "bundled up in blankets," he actually lives in an area that is usually warm. He lives with his mother. Because of the weather, he does not particularly care for living where he does because he perceives the weather to be "summer year around." Living up north also appeals to Eduardo because there "ain't millions of people" crowded into a small space.

Although he loves the idea of living in the cold, Eduardo does not actually like to be cold. He shivers frequently and asks that his hospital room temperature be raised from 70 to 85 degrees to ease his chilled body.

Shivering is a function of Eduardo's life in that he has a form of cancer called acute lymphocytic leukemia (ALL). He describes it as a "basic blood disorder." Although his initial diagnosis in the spring of 2001 came with what he was told was a "high rate of being cured," he relapsed two months prior to the interview.

Cancer is not new to Eduardo's family. When his parents divorced, Eduardo, an only child, said he had to move out. He did not elaborate why. He lived a big part of his life with his aunt who comes to see him frequently in the hospital. Two months before Eduardo was diagnosed with leukemia, his father died of liver and lung cancer.

Timing told Eduardo he was sick. He initially went to see a dentist because his mouth would not stop bleeding when he brushed his teeth. The dentist noticed a lot of bumps around Eduardo's neck and told him to go see a physician. "Then I was always tired; I was getting weak," Eduardo explained. Eduardo's dentist told him it was his lymph nodes. That night, he told his mom what the dentist said. She took him to a physician the very next day, Friday, where blood work was done. The medical staff told him to come back on Monday.

On Saturday, the physician's office staff called and asked that he come in immediately. Eduardo would have preferred waiting until the following Monday because he had plans for the weekend. When asked why he preferred waiting, Eduardo replied, "I'm just that type of person. I don't know. It wasn't really bothering me. I had dealt with it up until that time, so another couple of days won't really matter."

His mother prevailed, and she and Eduardo went back to the physician's office on Saturday. Eduardo remembers the physician's office was on the west side of the city. The physician was waiting for Eduardo, who was then transferred immediately to the emergency room of a local hospital.

"They already had a room, getting a room ready for us, and everything," he says. He knew something was very wrong.

Eduardo remembers being more "upset" than "scared."

"I was a little bit upset that I was sick, and they ruined my time," he explains. Since the initial diagnosis, Eduardo has lost more time to being sick with ALL, although he initially went into remission with hopes for a full recovery.

One of the first procedures Eduardo underwent because of his leukemia was a spinal tap. He remembers waking up during the procedure. He also remembers waking up during a bone marrow aspiration. "Yeah, it hurt," he says simply. Two months ago he was told cancer cells were found in his spinal fluid. Now Eduardo is going through more chemotherapy until a suitable bone marrow donor can be found.

He is also taking antibiotics for an infection that causes mucus buildup in the form of blisters in his throat. Both the throat infection and the need for more chemotherapy have necessitated Eduardo's most recent return to the hospital.

During this part of the conversation, a nurse walks into Eduardo's hospital room. He tells her he is busy right now.

"Do you want me to come back?" she asks.

"Yes, please," he responds. She turns and leaves the room. Eduardo runs his own show.

Talking about his illness with others is not something Eduardo likes to do. He finds talking about his situation, especially with his mother and aunt, frustrating because of the complicated nature of medical issues involving cancer.

"I don't really like to talk with them about it. They don't really understand. My aunt doesn't really understand, and she will get confused. She will start saying wrong things and telling other people different," he explains. He also believes that medical situations in general lend themselves to confusing talk. "It's really confusing if you don't know anything about it. Just the whole terminology and the ways things are called. And my aunt has that Mexican accent and a lot of things sound differently like that."

When asked if he remembers the specific language used by the physicians to tell him he was sick, he distinctly recalls the words he heard: "Hey Eduardo, you have leukemia."

Physicians then started "breaking it down, telling me I had ALL. It's acute lympho . . . leukemia, or something like that," he says. "I don't remember." After being given the initial diagnosis, Eduardo inquired little.

"I didn't really ask any questions. I just wanted to know if I could be cured or not. Because I didn't really want to know what it was."

Eduardo was told there was a high rate of being cured. Then he explains: "I just recently relapsed like two months ago." When I say, "I'm sorry," Eduardo replies, "Me, too."

Although he may not have wanted to know the full name of his disease when initially diagnosed, Eduardo is now acutely aware of what is being done to his body to try to keep him alive. He knows which intravenous bags are full of fluid, which are full of chemotherapy drugs, and which contain morphine. He is fully cognizant of which bags are being hung for him at which times, and why. He says he is feeling "pretty good" today because he is on morphine. "It takes the pain away," he explains.

Eduardo's recent relapse derailed his plans to start college in the fall. He is a high school graduate who hopes to attend a local community college and someday become a nurse. Before he got sick initially, he had his sights set on becoming a pediatrician. "But now that I'm here in the hospital, it takes longer to be a pediatrician," Eduardo says.

Hopefully in the next couple of days, Eduardo will be released from the hospital. When he gets home, he looks forward to watching cable television, channel surfing, and eating pizza or anything Italian. He loves rap and rhythm and blues music, or "whatever sounds good."

Eduardo converses easily about the movies he loves. *Finding Nemo* ("Ellen's crazy," he says referring to Ellen DeGeneres; and he loves her acting and being the voice of Dorie who speaks whale), *A Beautiful Mind, Radio,* and *The Titanic* are among his favorites. He suggests the film *A Beautiful Mind* is one you "can't see twice." When asked why, he replies: "Because you have already spoiled it by knowing the ending."

Eduardo says he is not certain as to the ending of his own story.

Interviewer: "Do you have an idea of how this is all going to work out?"

Eduardo: "Do I have an idea? No. I don't really know what is going to happen."

In the meantime, Eduardo continues to call things as he sees them. He focuses on what is real, as opposed to what may be imagined in a happenstance of hope.

"I'm not real optimistic. I'm pessimistic. I focus on the negative. Yeah, I've always been like that," he says.

He wishes other people would do the same. In fact, he resents people who hand him an optimistic view of his situation saying, "You are going to live, and everything is going to be alright." He goes on to explain, "You know how people tell you 'you are going to be alright. God has to know, you don't really know what is going to happen to you.'" Eduardo hates that kind of talk. He takes a more practical, authentic approach to his way of thinking.

"I focus more on the reality part of it—that I may die. And my life may come to an end. It just happens. I'm sure other people that pray and say that they are going to do OK don't end up living. That's mostly how it is," he says. When asked specifically if he wishes other people would talk to him using an optimistic or pessimistic point of view he replies:

"Pessimistic. I don't like it when they tell me what they think, and they tell me what they think like they know what is going to happen. And they tell you that you are going to be alright. You know how people are like, 'stay up,' saying that it is going to be alright. I always found it so corny. And now that I'm in the position, it sounds even more corny," he adds.

Eduardo continues to emphasize his perspective. As he is talking, I notice he changes his subject reference from "they" to "you" almost in midstream. Perhaps as he has continued his dialogue, he has switched from talking to me to talking directly to an imagined or remembered audience. "You (as opposed to they) don't know what my future holds. Don't talk to me like you do," he declares angrily.

Does he ever directly tell people not to talk to him in that way?

"No," he replies, "I just let them talk. I don't want to be rude or anything." He says he believes people who take an optimistic view of situations they are not directly living may think they are saying the right thing, but "they're just not."

Although Eduardo may hold strong feelings about how people should and should not talk with him, he is quick to place tight boundaries around how much talking he does with others. Not only does he prefer to remain silent in talking about his illness with his mom (because she cries a lot) and his aunt, he also prefers not to talk about his illness or his feelings with his friends.

"I wouldn't talk with anybody about it because most people don't want to hear what I have to say, because it's so negative."

His feelings are negative; they change very fast, and are oftentimes hard to pinpoint. When asked to describe how he feels emotionally, Eduardo responded with honest clarity about an ambiguous and unsettling situation:

"I don't know. Right now I feel good. But when I feel sick, it's like I think I'm going to die, it's just . . . it's not a good feeling what you go through."

Eduardo also has no interest in defining other people's stories, not even other young people who have cancer just like him.

Interviewer: "Is there anything you would say to parents of children, or young people, with cancer?"

Eduardo: "Me personally? No. Because you are going to feel the way you feel about it. And nobody can make you feel anything. . . . You don't know how other people feel. I mean, they can tell you, but at the end of the day you are still going to feel what you feel. So it doesn't really matter what anybody says. You have that mindset already."

Eduardo believes it would be hard for other young people to learn from him.

"I'm sure they are going through something worse than I'm going through. How do I talk to them? I don't want to say something that might hurt them, or that might get them thinking negative. I don't want to affect them like that," he explains.

Even though Eduardo does not talk much about his illness with anyone, he does pray at times, albeit infrequently.

"Sometimes I pray, but I didn't really pray before I got sick, so I don't really want to start praying now. I don't want to be one of those people who just comes to God when something bad happens," Eduardo explains. "Hypocrites," he calls them. "You know, like those people who only go to church on Easter and at Christmastime." Eduardo does not believe you have to go to church all the time. "Yeah, you don't, but damn. Yeah, but don't try to preach if you only go two times a year."

When Eduardo first got sick, he would lie in bed at night in the hospital. His mind would swirl.

"But I don't ask questions anymore, like *why?* Everything happens for a reason," he believes.

He understands that people may be afraid to use the word "death" around him because "deep down inside they might see that I may die. And they don't want to bring it up, which is perfectly fine with me. I don't really want to talk about it. I'm real to the fact that I may die, we've all got to die."

No longer does Eduardo feel a need to make full sense of his situation or behave a certain way or even talk to others. He is periodically bothered by the reality that leukemia is "just taking time out of my life that I can never get back because I would much rather be out there doing something else," he says.

When asked what the last few years have been like for him, Eduardo replies simply, "*There*. I'm still alive, so I guess they've been alright." When asked what could be worse than his present experiences, he replies, "Death and suffering. I haven't really been suffering. I'm in a much better position than a lot of other kids that have been here."

In the meantime, he continues to think about his life in terms of his philosophy that it is important to "just be patient, and let it play out. I don't want to rush it. Because it might not be what I want it to be."

Authenticity
An Interviewer's Perspective

A Lesson Learned - *Listening*

So much of what Eduardo had to say to me dealt
with what he didn't want others to say to him. He didn't
want people to tell him how to feel, or what to think, or
what they thought, or how things would work out, and
so on. Sometimes (and perhaps more times than not) to
be truly authentic and helpful, we must be *listening* as
opposed to doing all the talking.

**Suggested Response Strategies/Discussion Questions/
Commentary:**

** Practice silence. Sit with a friend and say or do
nothing for a time. Let the silence engulf you and
your surroundings. Learn to be personally comfortable with silence.

** Be intentional about trying to spend an hour or two
one day a week in complete silence as you go about
your business, if possible and practical.

** Watch peoples' body language, and analyze for yourself what it says to you. Try eating by yourself in a
restaurant or on a park bench and use the time for
observing human behavior around you as you listen
intently to noises and conversations.

** Watch your tendency to fill in conversational silence
gaps with words like *so, anyway, as I was saying.* Just
let some silence fill the air.

** Be upfront with someone who is seriously ill or dying
by saying something like: *I'm really not sure what is*

best to say right now, so I'd just like to be a good listener if you feel like talking. Then hush and truly start listening.

Your Personal Notes/Action Steps:

-7-

UNFILTERED HARRY

Twenty-year-old Harry sits on his front porch on a cold and gray Saturday afternoon in the fall of 2003. The afternoon in no way lends itself for anyone to be outside for any reason. It is damp and miserable. Not a single individual can be seen outside on the entire block. No birds are chirping, and the sky is void of color or character other than dreary. When I ask Harry if the cold might bother him because of his illness, he shot me a look that crossed between the inquisitive—*Have you always been stupid?*—and the cynical—*Who me? What have I got to lose?*

Harry is an incredibly direct yet courteous young man. He is also fast in sizing up his audience. When he realizes the weather might be too miserable for sitting outside for his company, he quickly asks if I want to talk inside. I say wherever he preferred. He sits down in a dirty plastic chair on his porch.

Then he asks if his smoking will bother me. Again I respond in a positive way by saying "Of course not," fully appreciating the fact that we are sitting on his front porch. Harry begins by saying he did not sleep very much the night before because he and his girlfriend drove a family member out of town to a camp for the autistic. The trip took almost all night. Yet Harry is gracious in keeping his interview appointment and giving a total stranger part of his time on a miserable Saturday afternoon.

Harry has lived with leukemia, acute lymphocytic leukemia (ALL), almost all his teenage years. He remembers first being diagnosed in the early part of 1998 when he was 14 years old. He knew something was wrong when the physician (in a "weird tone" that Harry knew meant bad news) asked his father to step outside the hospital room where Harry was undergoing tests. "If the physician can't say it in front of me, it can't be good. They weren't fooling anybody," Harry says.

At the time, Harry had never heard of ALL, but he had a vision about what the future meant in terms of the diagnosis.

"I never really knew what leukemia was. I just knew that you would be bald if you had it," he comments. Even after all these years, keeping track of his disease has not been easy. It seems like a never-ending on-again, off-again saga.

Harry battled leukemia and first went bald between 1998 and 2000. "Or 2001, maybe. Either 2000 or 2001," he tries to remember precisely; "2001, I think. And then I got over it, and it came back in 2002."

Harry is smart in a no-nonsense kind of way. He knows his long-term prognosis is not good, despite constant talk from his medical staff that he described as sugarcoating.

"They always tell me the good stuff, and it's come back twice already, and my chances are down to 50-50."

Harry knows there is a major potential wrinkle in his long-term life plan. Although he realizes his physicians and nurses "never tell me nothing bad, I figure when you've got a life-threatening illness, there's got to be some kind of catch somewhere," he says.

With that in mind, Harry made a pact with his physician whom he admires and heavily relies on. The pact is that if "he thought I wasn't going to make it," then he would answer me honestly. "What do you think from a professional point of view?" Harry would ask. "And he will always tell me, 'Well, I think it looks good.'"

Despite the pact, Harry understands things may not always be what they are set up to be. He recognizes the complexities and ambiguities often generating changes in people's good intentions, like honoring a pact, while communicating with individuals who may be at the end of their lives.

"But I think that's what the physician tells everybody. He's a doctor, that's what he's supposed to do, sugarcoat it all," Harry says.

Harry also believes the entire medical staff is adept at sidestepping his situation in a genuine effort to make him feel better.

"The first time I was diagnosed, they told me the same thing: 'It looks good,' and this and that. And now that I'm back, they tell me, 'Well, we kind of saw it back then when we thought it was going to go away, but there was some stuff that showed otherwise.'"

Even during this latest time when the staff was minimizing the situation, Harry saw reality.

"You know, the fact that my blood count didn't drop like it should, and they just had to stop injecting me when they reached the maximum they could be giving me, I knew that was a bad sign right there. All this time, my blood count is supposed to be lower because the chemo is supposed to be affecting the bad cells, and it's not for like a year," he recalls.

When asked if he perceives sugarcoating as a form of lying, Harry says, "No, because they tell me pretty much straightforward. If they told me, 'Well, look, you're going to live,' when I have a 50-50 chance, that's lying." But his physician told him, "'Look, you have a real serious disease again. It's really bad that you got it a second time.' That's not a really good sign at all. What that tells me is that the medicine is not working, which is very bad. You know, so he tells me the truth, that it's very bad."

When Harry was first diagnosed at age 14, he participated to a much lesser degree than now in conversations and decision making regarding his care.

"The real important stuff when I was 14, they would usually talk that over with my dad. They would kind of talk it over with him first, and then they would figure it out: 'OK, this is what we should tell him, and this is how we should tell him.'" Harry also remembers that the medical staff perceived him as having a greater *laissez-faire* attitude when he was younger, an incorrect assumption, he is quick to add. "I guess that when I was 14, I was always different in their eyes. Like I was always happy-go-lucky, so it didn't really bother me, you know?" But the staff was wrong, according to Harry. It did bother him to a greater degree than they realized.

"I mean, it did because it sucks, but other than that it would have been fine. I guess they figure that now that I am more of an adult, I can cope with the truth more than when I was younger," he adds.

Over the years, Harry has become adept at being more of a decision maker and conversationalist in his own health care situations. For the past two years, he has been going to the hospital by himself for treatments. Since he has been wrestling with leukemia for over six years, the routine of treatments, decisions, and medicines has become second nature to Harry.

"For me, it's like, OK, it's Monday. I'm going to the physician. I just get up and go about my business, like you would get up and go to school or work. Not like every day, but basically, pretty close to it. And if I wasn't in the hospital for chemo, I was in there for pneumonia or low blood counts, or, what's the word I'm looking for, neutropenia, when you have an unexplained fever and your blood counts are low. Just like it was my daily routine."

Harry is quick to express his appreciation to his medical staff. At times, he seems to rely more on them than his family. Although the process may frustrate him, he understands their reasoning for sugarcoating his situation by sometimes saying very little.

"If Dr. Carter doesn't really have any hard evidence, I'm thinking he's thinking about it. If he's not real sure that it's going to come back, why get me worried? As if I don't worry enough," Harry comments as he smiles wryly.

Harry believes his physician takes the long-term approach of just letting things ride for a while in an effort to help make life less of a worry for him. "Right now he says that everything is looking good. So, as long as nothing is showing up bad, there is really no reason for him to say nothing to me anyway."

Harry's odds of long-term survival are continuing to worsen. They will not get better. At a minimum, he hopes, over time his body will stop the current statistical spiral downward from his initial diagnosis of 70-30 (70 percent cure/30 percent return rate) to his current odds of 50-50. If his leukemia returns for a third time, however, his odds will drop even further to 30-70 (30 percent cure/70 percent return rate). As his odds have worsened, so has the talk and language associated around his disease— or at least how he perceives them.

"It's kind of like the first time that everybody made it sound like a breeze, which I guess it was supposed to be because I had a 70-30 chance, so I guess it was supposed to be pretty simple. Since they made it out to be so simple, like, I went through it and once I finished my last treatment, in my mind, that was it, OK cool, I'm over it. Live my life as a normal person now.

"And then a year later, I got a job. I got everything going. I got car payments, just like any adult would. And then it just comes back out of nowhere, and I'm like, Man, it came back, how does that happen? Wait a minute. It's not supposed to do that. Seventy-thirty means it don't come back. Kind of jumps up and slaps you in the face.

"And you realize that it does come back. My mentality about it is: I had a 70-30 that didn't work. Now I have a 50-50. If your luck ain't good enough for a 70-30, you really ain't going to make a 50-50. And then if it comes back again, he [his physician] said that I drop down, he said to, probably under a 30-70."

Harry is also extremely frustrated with the ambiguity that comes with 50-50 odds.

"Fifty-fifty doesn't tell me much. That's another thing. Not only do my odds suck, it doesn't really tell me anything. You know, if I had a 20 percent or a 10 percent or a 30 percent even, then I would pretty much know what to look forward to. Now I'm kind of like, well shit, what's going to happen, am I going to make it, or am I not going to make it? What's going on?"

Yet he is resolute at times. "If I go through my life thinking I'm going to die, then obviously, no matter how strong-willed you are, you're going to. It's going to affect you. So I just try to stay strong until they tell me otherwise."

If Harry's odds continue downward and the ALL comes back again, he anticipates having some very tough decisions to make, like undergoing a bone marrow transplant. The side effects of transplantation can be "really horrible," he says, especially "if I find out that I have a 1 percent chance." Side effects that worry Harry include skin graphing, where "your skin falls off." He also mentions platelet dependency, where "every day you have to go in there and get infusions of platelets, like everything. So you don't even really have a normal life anyway. *What else?*" he asks himself. "All kinds of stuff. Yeah—like all kinds of stuff. Real bad horrible stuff that I had never heard of or that I had never thought about because nobody had ever told me.

"But then again, that's their job because they aren't really supposed to talk me out of getting whatever additional treatment I may need should the cancer return. They are supposed to try to talk me into any hope there is. You know what I mean? If there is the slightest bit of hope, they are supposed to talk me into going for it."

People marvel at Harry's ability to stay upbeat amidst his life situation. People say to him repeatedly, "You're never depressed?"

"And what I always tell everybody is, I'm like, 'If I'm depressed, would that cure me?' That would just give me a miserable life along with a deadly disease. Two wrongs don't make a right. I'm not going to be able to fix it, so I might as well enjoy my life the best I can.

"I tell everybody that. I say it's not going to cure anything by me being depressed or sad about it or me dwelling on it. I might as well live my life the best I can and be as happy as I can while I'm here, you know, and appreciate these people who are with me. And if I'm depressed, you know, what is that going to do? It's going to make my dad depressed. It's going to make my girlfriend depressed. The kids are going to be depressed. My whole family, you know what I mean? My outlook, I think, that's the reason why they have a good outlook on it, and . . . because I go through it with such ease, kind of, it's like, they don't really even get sad. They see how I'm strong, and they say, 'Oh yeah, he's going to make it.' You know what I mean?"

Harry uses the word "weird" a lot. He uses it in terms of how he thinks about life in general, including his own. He uses it to describe how people talk to him, around him, about him, and down to him. He especially thinks about the way in which public policy and political decisions are made regarding research for his disease.

"I don't think they have enough research going on for leukemia. Like I just heard on the news the other day they spent, like a billion dollars or like a hundred million dollars on figuring out about Alzheimer's. I figure, that's cool, I mean, I'm really glad that you are going to make a lot of older people remember stuff they forgot. But meanwhile, you got 2-, 3-, 4-, 5-year-old children dying every day. What about them?"

The weirdness and irony in Harry's mind is not just placed in the public arena. It is also personal. He knows the 2-, 3-, 4- and 5-year-old children who are dying and for whom he lobbies.

"And that's pretty hard to deal with, too, because I am pretty good friends with a patient who just passed away. Not so long ago, I went to his funeral, his viewing. I still hang out with his family, and so it's kind of rough to deal with. I've seen a ten-year-old boy get turned into an only child from diseases like this. So it's kind of hard to deal with. Like, I've seen the same case with my friend, his parents now only have—they *had* two boys; now they only have one boy. You know, like, imagine, you grow up with just you and one sibling, and then all of a sudden, you're by yourself. They get taken from you. It's kind of weird."

Harry prays more now than he used to in an attempt to curb some of his anger. When he was young and "a lot more immature," he says, "I kind of had that attitude of God did it so I'm mad at Him." Now he thinks he is smarter. "It's like when you're little, you know, and your parents don't let you get something. Well, telling them something, getting rude with them is not going to help you any. You know what I mean? So you might as well be nice," he philosophizes. "Now I've gotten more into praying instead of being mad."

Yet he is particular about what he prays for at this time in his life.

"Usually I'm not a very selfish person at all, like if you knew me you would know that. So the usual way that I pray is like to let me be healthy and to keep me around. But if He doesn't, I know that there is a reason that I probably don't know, but that I will find out when

I get up there, wherever I'm going. I'll probably find it out. But I just tell them that, you know, if He does end up taking me, just to make sure that my family is OK."

In the meantime, he is still wondering about his future in terms of where he will end up. "Yeah, show me," he challenges. "Who can tell me, 'Oh, I've been there; Heaven's the coolest place around, you know, it's happening!' Nobody can tell you that.

"All you know is that there are a hundred old books about people who used to get all high off something and write down stuff. That's all it is," he says, referring to books and philosophies about Heaven as described in the Bible. "Who's to tell you what those people were on back then? You know? They were on acid or something. Yeah, there's this guy, he's in the sky, I've seen him."

Harry also wonders about Hell, especially since he says he has made some "bad choices" in his life. "They can't let everybody in [referring to Heaven], so there's got to be some [referring to Hell]. Everybody always tells me, 'All you've got to do is ask for forgiveness for any bad things you've ever done, and you'll get right in.' If it were that easy, Hell would go out of business. The devil would get out and become an angel again," he argues. Harry suggests many of us make our own Hell on earth.

"The way people live their life is a big part of it. Like I said, a lot of people would feel like this is Hell, you know—the worst, going through a real bad disease. But I make the best of it. I still got the people I love, you know what I mean? Knock on wood. There's wood lying around here somewhere," he says, searching.

Of all the phrases used in a cancer hospital with seriously ill young people, the one Harry hates the most is "quality of life."

"I don't like that term, it makes me sound like a used car. Quality of life. That means my resale value isn't too much, kind of, you know?"

He remembered the phrase was used repeatedly, especially when he was younger. "I don't remember how they used it, but I remember them using the term quality of life. What does that mean, my life sucks, what are you trying to say? What does that mean? My life is not worth living? Fill me in. Explain it to me slower. I'm 14 now. Come on now," he had challenged.

"I don't know, it just gets to me. It's nothing fancy, but to a five year old or a fourteen year old, they might think *Well, what is that?* And a lot of time when they used to tell me that, I used to just skip right over it and not think about it. I would just go on about my thing because I didn't understand it."

Harry is suspicious, if not cynical, about death. He is suspicious about the notion of Heaven as an end-all nirvana. The hospice chaplains reminded him that God is not fair, and that life is not fair. They asked him to think about things in ways that are not always easy for him, like "everything happens for a reason, and that in the Bible it says that everybody is supposed to go through trials and tribulation and suffering," he says. He is not certain about the logic or comfort that comes from hearing such words.

He is also still puzzled about the loss of life at such a young age. Ironically, he is not referring to himself, although he was only 14 when first diagnosed, but rather to those much younger children with cancer whose situations seem to crawl under his skin, given their injustices and insanities.

One day the hospice chaplain asked Harry how he knew that a five year old passing away was such a bad thing. "This kind of struck me. It kind of upset me at first, but then the chaplain went on to explain by saying, 'How do you know that God's not actually God, because, at five years old, God's taken them to Heaven? You know he's not going to get judged or anything, he's just going to go straight up to Heaven.' Even if he did get judged, it is obvious where he would go, because he was the sweetest boy, and the chaplain said, 'You know he's going to go to Heaven because he's five years old,' " Harry recalls.

The hospice chaplain challenged Harry to think about death in a different way. Harry remembered the chaplain asking him, "How do you know that God is not actually saving him from something bad going on in his life?" The question certainly made Harry think. In fact, Harry thinks the only plausible explanation for why young children die from illnesses like his is maybe because they are being saved from something bad that was going to happen.

"You never know what would have happened in a young child's life, if he would have lived," he says. Yet he still remains unsure.

"See, that's the thing, too. I kind of have mixed feelings about it. I've gone through a lot of rough stuff in my life, the leukemia, a bunch of other stuff, you know, I've had a pretty rough life. And, you know, everybody says that 'Oh, Heaven is the perfect place, it's paradise,' this and that. That's probably true, but to me, it's not. I don't think that it's the perfect place. Just because of the fact that it may be the perfect place in the end, but to me, even though I have been through so much, this is the

perfect place for me. I love my family; I love my environment; I love the people around me."

Harry firmly believes cancer patients initially have
few choices. They are bound by a practical reality, sug-
gesting a need to reach out and grab hold of whatever
treatment is offered to them. He thinks this is especially
true of the younger cancer patients whose treatment
decisions are being made by their parents. "They don't
have no choice," he says. In that process, those younger
patients and their parents inspire the 20-year-old Harry.

"There's nothing amazing about me," he suggests.
"Just to be able to go through it is amazing. Those
patients down there in the palliative care center area for
the younger patients, they inspire me. I don't think I
would have made it all through my treatment if it
wasn't for seeing all those little kids and stuff."

Being a role model to the younger patients is something that has always been important to Harry although
he is not sure he is particularly up for the challenge.

"When I was inpatient, I kind of felt that I had to be a
role model for those kids. You know what I mean?
Granted, I never came out of my room because I was too
busy throwing up, but I always felt, just being there, you
know, they see an older person being there, they feel
like, *Man, look at him, he's older. I want to be older, too.* They
kind of look at it, and they try and be stronger, because
they see somebody older in there, and they want to be
older. They want to be my age someday."

Harry feels the same about his own family. Harry's
father is his role model.

"That's kind of what keeps me going, too, because I
see my dad, and I want to be a grandfather one day. I
want to go through all that stuff."

Almost every example of a young cancer patient Harry mentions specifically refers to a five-year-old boy. That little five-year-old boy Harry thinks about almost all the time is his friend, Lucas. Harry worships Lucas. Lucas is Harry's role model. The only time in a several-hour interview that Harry came even close to crying was when he talked about Lucas. Cancer killed little Lucas. Harry talked to one of the hospice chaplains about Lucas in his ongoing attempts to make sense of things.

"It was more of a religious talk than anything else. I told the chaplain, 'I don't seem to understand.' I was like, 'You hear on the news about people robbing banks and stuff, they get shot three or four times in the head, and they still live and get out of jail a year later. And you've got the sweetest little boy I've ever met in my whole life—a five-year-old boy, sweetest little boy you'll ever meet in your life," he says again. "He is so sweet. And he just dies. You know what I mean? I just don't think it's fair." Harry is firmly convinced Lucas "got gypped."

"You know, all the fun stuff that we take for granted, he never got a chance to do. He never got a chance to just make his own decisions. You know? You wake up on your day off or something, and you are like *where am I going to go today? What am I going to do?* Nobody's telling you what to do because you are not five years old. You just go about your day, wherever you want to go, you go. If you want to get in your car right now and drive to Canada, you'll do it, just because you want to. And he never got to drive a car. Have a girlfriend. Go to high school. Actually have a group of friends that he went out and had fun with. He never got to do nothing," he laments.

Harry's eyes well up with tears. They glisten beyond the smoke from his cigarette. He looks away and shifts his body forward in the patio chair, as if to push the tears back into his face. Harry has not cried once before, not even when talking about the prospects of his own death.

Harry rhetorically pushes the envelope. He does not mince words. He is like the movie character Dirty Harry. He tells it like it is. You keep waiting for him to snarl, "*Make my day.*" He is also direct in saying what he needs. He thinks cancer patients like himself, especially those who are younger, need to hear "more reassurance from the physician that everything is going to be fine." And yet he does not say in particular what that reassurance might entail. Does it mean being cured, living a long time, being less sick today than tomorrow, finding a suitable bone marrow donor? Harry does not elaborate.

Harry suggests reassurance is the most important message needing to be conveyed to people who are possibly staring at the end of their lives. He is also especially adamant that such reassurances need to be conveyed over and over again to younger patients with life-threatening illnesses.

In thinking about how to tell people they have cancer, Harry pontificates. "I think, as you get older, unless it's a baby or somebody really, really young who really doesn't know much, I think the older you get, the easier it would probably be to tell somebody. I think when you are five, it's real hard to.

"But then again, when you're older, you can tell a five-year-old boy he has cancer, and he's like, *OK.*"

Then Harry pauses, as if to wonder about the theory that ignorance is bliss.

"A five-year-old patient doesn't know what he's in for. But if you break it down for him and tell him, 'Look, you have this disease called cancer. It's probably going to end up killing you. But if it doesn't kill you, you are going to wish it did because you are just going to end up spending year after year throwing up in the hospital.' But other than that, I don't think that a five year old can really understand what's going on. You know what I mean?

"And then it would be more of a thing, well, let me tell him so that at least he knows. He may not understand exactly, and then once he starts going through treatment, he starts feeling weird and stuff. Then try to be his best friend. Try to talk to him and be real friendly with him so he trusts you. And just be straightforward with him," he adds.

Harry also believes delivery is important. Pauses are suspect, along with weird tones from the physicians, although he cannot fully describe what qualifies as a weird tone.

"Just the way my physician said that my cancer had returned, you could tell bad news was coming." Harry gives an example: "'Well, Harry, I would like to tell you that, uh [pause].' You know, when somebody keeps pausing, it's not a good thing that's happening."

When he found out his cancer had returned after experiencing severe headaches at work, Harry recalls receiving the news.

"They looked at my blood and told me I had it again. And they go, 'OK, well, we've got a room saved for you

on the inpatient side, and we need you to start tonight.'"
Harry protested.

"The disease needs me to start tonight on chemo?
Well, the disease can wait until tomorrow. That doesn't
meet up with my schedule. I don't feel like starting
tonight. I'm not going to live my life depending on what
I need to do to beat that disease. It's not going to work,"
he told the medical staff and his family, many of them
crying softly. "Either the disease is going to work my
way, or it is just not going to work, and that's just not the
way it was meant to be. I told my doctor that I wanted to
go home and think about it. I was like, I don't even know
if I want to go through this again," he adds.

Harry went home that night for time to "count his
blessings" and "see why I'm going to put myself through
all of that trouble again," he says. Later that night he
went out and partied with friends. In the end, he decided
to start treatments again largely on the advice of his
physician and the nursing staff at the cancer hospital.

"I've been going there so long, I trust them. If my
doctor tells me there is nothing wrong, then nothing's
wrong. If Ted [one of his favorite oncology nurses] tells
me he thinks that I'm going to get cured, then that's
what I'm going to believe. They've just built up that
trust with me. You know, everybody down there has.
They've made it to where, as far as I know, they've never
just lied to my face. They've sugarcoated stuff in the
past like I said, but that's their job, they're supposed to
do that."

Harry also distinguishes between talking in a
straightforward manner, as opposed to a cut-throat
manner, to use his words.

"Cut-throat? No. Not to a five year old. I was just saying . . . that's what you would have to say for them to understand exactly what they are going to go through. Because you tell a five-year-old boy that he has cancer, 'you've got ALL-leukemia,' he's going to look at you like, 'Is that good? Do I get some candy or a toy?' They're not going to understand exactly what that is. But you tell a 20 year old, *you got cancer*, they are like, 'Aw, shit.' You know what I mean? They are like, 'Damn,'" he says.

When Harry was first told he had cancer at age 14, he says he just "kind of laughed about it. It wasn't serious to me, but then again, I didn't really know what I was in for either. And that's one thing I think: Cancer really sucks. Because, most diseases and stuff, you know how to get rid of them. You take antibiotics or some-thing that makes you feel better. Because usually you have a disease that medicine makes you feel better.

"Well, with cancer, you've got a disease that makes you feel like crud, and they give you something that makes you feel even worse, a lot worse. That's kind of how I think you get ripped off. Any other thing, your treatment makes you feel better. This thing, your treat-ment just, it's kind of like, in a fight, the leukemia knocks you on the ground, and then the chemo just kind of gives you those last few kicks while you're laying there."

As the interview draws to a close, Harry stubs out the last of many cigarettes. The cold, damp air seems worse now because it is late afternoon. The sky remains dark. Harry thinks again of little Lucas, his role model.

"To be honest, Lucas inspired me more than I inspired him, I think. He went through it, then he relapsed, too, so he went through what I went through, too, if not worse. I think he really went through worse honestly. Actually, I know he went through a lot worse," he clarifies. "How am I going to be scared or not willing to do something that a five-year-old boy does? That's another reason that I began treatments again. I'm figuring, if these children can go through it without a say-so, then so can I. They don't have the say-so of whether they want to or not; they are made to go through it.

"It's kind of like when you are in the army, you stick up for your army. When you're a police officer, you stick up for other police officers. If there are little kids dying every day, and they went through everything they could, and they still pass away, you never know. I would hate to give up on it, and then find out—when I get to Heaven or whatever, that if I didn't give up on it, I would have lived, because to me that would have made me feel like that small.

"Because I don't think that it would be right for somebody my age to give up such a wonderful opportunity to continue their life when there are people who get that life taken from them, they have no choice. And I figure that, I think, that's the most horrible thing I could do, from my position, is just give up an opportunity that I'm given.

"As far as now, even if I do die, I still have time. I would at least probably say a year or two. Worst-case scenario, you know, I'm open." With that, he proceeded to introduce me to his girlfriend's young children. "You could imagine what it would be like to lose a father, especially at a young age," he says, thinking of his own family.

For more than two solid hours, this young man, who knew at age 14 he would periodically be bald and sick because of leukemia, has told the story of his life for the last six years. The good, the bad, and the ugly. He has spoken with the utmost candor. He has asked many tough questions and challenged many perceptions that come with few clear answers.

Many of Harry's viewpoints, feelings, and pontifications are mixed and contradictory. Without a doubt, they are all frank and raw. He is incredibly generous in giving of his time in order to help other people through the telling of his own story. There is a sense in which he seems to be wondering why he is still alive, and his dear five-year-old friend, little Lucas, is dead.

For now, Harry lives with an internal view of abundance and gratefulness.

"For the most part, my suffering has come from the chemo and stuff, you know what I mean? And that just has to do with me, and like I said, I'm not a selfish person. So if that's what I have to look forward to, my pain and suffering during life, then I'll take it with a grain of salt, and just be thankful that my family is OK. Because, that's the only thing I'm worried about is, the people I love. I'm pretty strong willed, too. I can pretty much go through anything. I can go through six years of this stuff, you know. I don't think there's anything out there I can't do," he says convincingly.

In the meantime, he will make the most of every single day that comes his way.

"And if God does take me young, then I enjoyed what I had. That's just the way it is," Harry says.

Driving back from the interview, I was reminded for some reason of the song from *Carousel* that comedian

Jerry Lewis sings at the end of each annual Muscular Dystrophy Association (MDA) fund-raising telethon. It begins:

> *"When you walk through a storm, hold your head*
> *up high*
> > *And don't be afraid of the dark."*

Perhaps from Harry, the message is somewhat similar: When you walk through a storm, tell it like it is. Make my day, Unfiltered Harry.

Epilogue

Unfiltered Harry lost his third battle with cancer in 2005. His physician said he went down fighting.

Unfiltered Harry
An Interviewer's Perspective

A Lesson Learned – *Telling the Truth*

Never shall I forget my afternoon with Unfiltered Harry for so many reasons, mainly because of the remarkable young man he is and his incredible ability at *telling the truth* in the specific way it was for him. There is tremendous freedom in being unfiltered and not spending countless amounts of energy or time sugar-coating or avoiding or mis-characterizing bad situations. Harry knew his time on earth was limited; so he went about telling the truth for him: the good, the bad and the ugly.

Suggested Response Strategies/Discussion Questions/ Commentary:

** If you are dealing with someone with a serious or terminal illness who is coherent and able to converse, be brave and ask him or her how best to talk about the situation at hand. Take your cue from the person who is ill. Learn from him or her.

** Tell the truth during these tough times, in whatever form you perceive those truths to be, and in whatever ways you deem most appropriate and helpful to yourself and others.

** Ask medical/hospice professionals to tell you what might happen in the near future, if you want to know. If you don't want to know, make that known as well.

Your Personal Notes/Action Steps:

WAITING

In the Butterfly Room of a children's hospital cancer ward, Corazon sits waiting and watching. She sits alone in the small living room adjacent to her son's hospital bed. Her son, six-year-old Marcelo, fidgets in the bed nearby, seemingly watching cartoons. There is only a muffled sound coming from his television.

Marcelo is extremely restless. His eyes, although sunk deep into his face, are open. His stares are piercing and haunting when you smile and say hello. He does not smile back.

Both eyes are blackened from internal bleeding. His lips are chapped and the skin is cracked and torn. He does not smile, but groans periodically in low tones. His mother leans down closer to his body and softly asks, "*Mijito*" (son) "are you hurting?" He says no, yet continues to squirm in bed. With his emaciated legs, he tosses his white bed sheet on and off his rail-thin body. He is bleeding from the lips, along with many other parts of his body as his medical staff explains later. He continues to moan.

At age six, time is slipping away for Marcelo. Perhaps his groans suggest he is aware of the intensity and brevity of his situation. Maybe he is angry. Or perhaps he is in pain, despite the morphine drip that hangs nearby and despite what he has just told his mom. Perhaps all of the above.

I wonder if the presence of a third unknown party in the room, despite Corazon's approval, is making a bad situation worse. When I offer to leave, Corazon quietly responds, "It's okay." She wants to tell her story and give voice to her dying son who is too ill to talk.

Many hospice programs or pediatric cancer centers like the one that Marcelo is in have what are called Butterfly Rooms or programs. The rooms represent areas for transitioning from this life to the next, much like the morphing of a cocoon into a butterfly.

Butterfly Rooms are usually decorated in bright yet soothing colors, similar to the room in which Corazon and Marcelo are located. Butterfly Rooms are usually much larger than traditional hospital rooms and are designed to accommodate entire families with separate living areas, kitchenettes, pull-out couches, and other items. To say that someone is in a Butterfly Room ordinarily means he or she is getting ready to die.

On this particular Friday afternoon, Corazon and Marcelo are alone in the Butterfly Room suite. No family members are huddled nearby. The two rooms that join together to make the room are cheerful and bright. Yet everything is quiet and seems to move at a slow pace. Marcelo's groans are quiet. Corazon speaks quietly. Medical staff personnel come and go, softly and unobtrusively. Corazon sits, waits, and watches while she tells her story.

Corazon and Marcelo, whom she watches from across the room, are both beautiful. Their eyes are dark, expressive, and sad. They both have dark hair and are extremely youthful despite the weariness showing on their faces.

Corazon sits by herself in the living area of the Butterfly Room. Like her son, she is watching another television with the sound barely on. She is watching a segment from *Oprah* in which a husband in Florida is appealing to the court of public opinion to end his wife's life. She says the show takes her mind off of Marcelo's situation. At the risk of inadvertently placing wrongful judgment on the husband in Florida, who is doing what he views as best for his family, I am struck by the irony. Here a young mother sits helplessly alone, watching a television show about a person actively pursuing death for a loved one, while her own son lies dying in the next room. Her conversation with me over the next hour suggests she would do anything to make things different for her son.

Marcelo is Corazon's first-born child. As if life were not challenging enough with Marcelo's situation, Corazon's other younger son, Marcelo's brother, has severe autism.

Corazon distinctly remembers the day in the fall of 2001 when she was told Marcelo had cancer. She was alone at the time.

"It wasn't what I was expecting. Being your first-born. He was never sick at the time. It was very scary," she explains. Her eyes well up with tears, but she does not make a sound.

Marcelo has lived for the past two years with a form of cancer called neuroblastoma. The National Cancer Institute and Cancer Index describe neuroblastoma as one of the most common solid tumors of early childhood that is usually found in babies or young children, with two-thirds of the cases occurring in children younger than five years of age. The disease usually originates in some area of the nervous tissue, the most common site of which is the abdomen. It can also be found in the chest, neck, pelvis, and other body areas.

Most neuroblastoma patients have widespread disease upon initial diagnosis. Approximately 70 percent of all patients with the disease have metastatic (or spreading) disease at diagnosis. For children of any age whose evidence of the disease is localized, as opposed to spreading, and for infants younger than one year of age with advanced illness, there is a high likelihood of long-term survival from the disease. Survival chances for older children with advanced-stage neuroblastoma are significantly decreased, however, despite intensive therapy. As an example, the National Cancer Institute reports a two-year survival rate of approximately 20 percent in older children with end-stage neuroblastoma.

When physicians initially told Corazon that Marcelo had neuroblastoma, they used what she described as little words, the words mass and tumor. They did not initially use the word neuroblastoma.

"They showed me how Marcelo had a tumor the size of two fists in his abdomen." (She holds up her fists to show the large size). "He's a very petite little boy," she says. The physician explained to Corazon that the mass in Marcelo's stomach was not supposed to be there.

In the Hispanic culture, much is written about the strong matriarchal role of women. Such seems to be the case in this family. Corazon's husband, Marcelo's father, was working at the time the news about Marcelo was delivered. One of the hardest parts of the initial ordeal for Corazon was telling her husband about their son.

"That was hard because he lost his mom like a year and a half before to cancer," she says softly. She looks away and down at her lap, as if to hide extremely painful memories. There also seems to be an unstated projection from her that somehow she has let her family down because of the multiple deaths.

At first, Corazon and her husband asked few, if any, questions.

"You kind of just stay stunned, in shock, I guess. And then you kind of say, 'well, what should we do, what is there to do?' And then they sit down with you and tell you: 'These are your chances. And this is what is going to take place. He will get sick from chemo.' They are very straightforward with you," she recalls.

Corazon appreciates the candor of the medical staff, despite the pain of the message.

"We had a conference, and we asked, you know, 'what are his possibilities of getting better?' And you know, it was told to us, 10 to 20 percent, that he might. You know, that's a very small amount," she says. "But we had some hope, but I think deep inside you are kind of like, 'Oh, okay.' Kind of trying to get the reality in there. But it takes time."

The initial treatments were the hardest on everyone, especially Marcelo and Corazon.

"The first time it's really bad, because by the second day, he has the nausea. And then to see him, because he's so petite. The first session, because you hear of the nausea and you are like, 'Oh, he didn't get it the first day.' But then the second day, 'I'm going to throw up,'"

Corazon recalls Marcelo saying. By the second session, Marcelo began losing his hair.

"It was on his pillow, and he was kind of like, 'Why is my hair falling out?' I'm like, 'Well, you know—,' " she adds.

For his mom, one of the hardest parts of Marcelo's journey over these past two years is watching his body physically waste away. Marcelo has always been small. At age four before he became ill, he already weighed approximately ten pounds less than national parenting statistics suggest an average four year old weighs. He continues to drop well beyond the national averages on a daily basis. In fact, Marcelo's frame unfortunately looks like that of a little old man.

Another of the biggest challenges faced by Corazon relates to what to say to her son. While she appreciates the directness of the medical staff, she struggles with putting reality into words for Marcelo. As conversations have taken place over these past two years, Marcelo has created his own visual images of what he is being told.

"And that's the other thing, explaining to him what is going on," she says. Her eyes fill up with tears that she quickly wipes away. She is careful not to make a sound other than the low tones of her voice.

"He wasn't in the room when I was told he had cancer. I had to tell him later, and it's hard to explain. You know, he turned five just recently so, to a five year old, to tell him, 'You have cancer.' And he's like, 'What's that, is that what's making me puke?'" she recalls Marcelo asking.

Corazon explained to Marcelo, "There's little rocks in your body, baby, and they are in different places. And they are not supposed to be there. It's called cancer. And he himself said, 'it seems like the devil.' We're Catholic, it's mostly like, we haven't gone to church in a long time because of Manual (her young son with autism). You can't take an autistic little boy to church on Sundays. It's like one parent has to watch him. You know, so it's very hard. So, where Marcelo got that? (she shrugs with a smile), 'It's like the devil?'" she repeats with wonder. With that, she asks to stop the interview briefly in order to get Marcelo some chocolate. He continues to groan, but says he needs or wants nothing.

For many years Corazon has had a lot on her plate. She seems to be a very strong and caring individual. When she was a small child, she took care of her parents, both of whom were ill. Her mother later became afflicted with cirrhosis of the liver, although ironically she recalls, "my dad drank, which was odd."

The last few years of her life have been extremely challenging for Corazon. The spring of 2001 was when Manuel was diagnosed with severe autism. Times were incredibly hard.

Later that same year, Marcelo was diagnosed with cancer. In the spring of the following year, Corazon's mother became acutely ill and in need of liver and kidney transplants. She eventually survived. During her mother's illness, the petite Corazon cared for the incontinent woman, "a big woman, just big everywhere," in her home along with her two boys, one with autism and the other with neuroblastoma.

The scene was not pretty, nor sanitary, an important medical element in the environmental lives of struggling cancer patients.

"I was a Clorox and Lysol freak; it was very hard," Corazon recalls. Corazon is also currently raising her sister's oldest daughter who is about the same age as Marcelo.

Throughout his illness, Marcelo has not talked very much, although he can be talkative at times. He has asked only once about the devil, yet he does continue to ask questions, as would any curious six year old. He wonders if the female hospice chaplain is the Lady God. His mom tells him that although she isn't God, she is the hospice chaplain and does know God. That seems to have pleased Marcelo, as Corazon recalls.

Corazon also recalls that the more the hospice chaplain would visit him, the more Marcelo would ask about God, and what God was doing. Corazon once told Marcelo that "God was in him."

"Again I ran into that problem where I am not the expert, so, you know, I'll kind of say what I think is right," she explains. Such dialogue gives way to interesting questions from Marcelo. Marcelo has asked his mom if she thinks God is in his stomach. "Do you think He's eating my hamburger?" he used to say.

"He'll say, 'I think He drank my punch because I'm thirsty again.' Just things like that. He would say, 'Well, he's probably thirsty. He could take a drink in my stomach, that's okay.' "

One of the reasons Corazon believes her son prefers not to talk very much is because he is shy around strangers. She believes over time he has changed his perspective on the medical personnel who deliver his chemotherapy.

"When we first started chemotherapy, he was talking to everybody. But then he found out that when he's in the hospital, he gets sick with his chemo. So I guess in his mind, these people are making him sick, and they are talking to him. 'So I'm not going to talk to them.' " She speculates about what Marcelo might be thinking. "He told me at home, he goes, 'they want to hear me talk, and I'm not going to talk to them.'" Corazon recognizes her son has what she calls *attitude*. "So, when we would come here to the hospital, he would just close his lips." When the medical staff asked him something, Marcelo would seldom respond.

"He would say, 'I don't want them to hear me talk. They're not going to hear my voice.' So he had that attitude. . . . He had that thing where he wasn't going to talk to anybody."

Corazon and her son seem to worship each other. From across the width of the Butterfly Room, they seemingly connect with each other, with few words ever being exchanged. Corazon is extremely cautious about how she behaves in front of Marcelo.

"He might have gotten a little bit of that attitude from me, but you know, he was a very happy-go-lucky kind of guy." Corazon now thinks part of what resulted in Marcela telling her he would not talk means that sometimes he only talks to the medical staff when she is not in the room.

"I don't know if he's like, 'I already told my mom I'm not talking, so I've got to keep my honor.' Even with the nurses, he would talk to some of them, but as soon as I would walk in, he wouldn't talk."

Marcelo's cancer pain is physically bad. He requires a great deal of morphine to minimize the discomfort. Sometimes his groans suggest the morphine is not working, as he continues to thrash in his bed. Marcelo's emotional discomfort is always very bad when he sees his mother cry.

"Marcelo doesn't want me to cry. If he hears me, he just gets hysterical. He gets mad, and he starts to cry, and he says, 'Stop crying!' He loses it, he just loses it. So, it's like, it's hard because I have to keep that straight face with him. Sometimes I just can't," she adds quietly, with tears filling her eyes. She looks down and away from Marcelo.

Marcelo has told his mother that he believes both God and the devil are in his stomach, and that God is fighting the devil, which is the cancer. At times he asks her, "What happens if the devil wins?" She tells him that "the cancer will win, and that you are probably going to die and go to Heaven."

Marcelo has seemed to worry not only about his own future but also about the futures of the other children he knows who have cancer like him. Corazon is convinced that at times her son has pretended to be asleep, but he's been listening to the nurses and physicians in his room and to other parents. Later he would ask his mom about what he had heard, like "All these kids have cancer. Are all of them going to die?"

Corazon does not hesitate to use the word *death* in front of Marcelo if she believes that straight talk is in order. Humor is important within the family in that sometimes family members will tell Marcelo that even after he gets to Heaven, he can come back to earth and turn off the television sets so that no one will be able to see their favorite shows.

"He'll say to his cousin, 'I'm going to go take out the cables when you are watching *Kim Possible* (a favorite television show). Yeah, I'm going to take them all out, and you're not going to be able to see it,' " his mom recalls.

Sometimes Marcelo asks Corazon directly, "Mommy, am I going to Heaven?" He will ask her to explain once again what Heaven is. Then the six year old will respond, "Well, I don't want to go to Heaven right now. Maybe tomorrow."

Epilogue

After this interview was conducted, Marcelo unexpectedly regained enough strength to leave the Butterfly Room and return home with his mom. He lived several more tomorrows; he died one month later.

Waiting
An Interviewer's Perspective

A Lesson Learned – *Giving Voice*

Those of us around unresponsive dying people hold an incredible opportunity for *giving voice* to them, as Corazon did for her son while sitting in the Butterfly Room. Ask yourself these questions: is there anyone depending on you to speak? What should you be saying, and to whom?

Suggested Response Strategies/Discussion Questions/ Commentary:

** Try to communicate as much as possible with your loved one so wishes and desires are known before someone becomes unresponsive.

** When unresponsive times occur, think about how you are going to give voice to your loved one. What are the answers to the questions above?

** Think about giving public voice to your loved one by speaking at his or her funeral. If you do not think you could take on such an undertaking, write out your thoughts and ask someone to communicate the message.

** Write your own personal obituary and make your own funeral plans long before you die. Communicate the steps you have taken and the plans you want to your loved ones.

** Think about how you want to make your final messages known to others. Consider writing personal letters to loved ones to be read either before or after you die. Put them in a secure place for safekeeping.

** Consider carrying out the voices of those who have died before us through scholarships, donations, property enhancements, mementos, etc.

** Make your voice heard loud and clear, throughout and especially during the ending times of your life.

Your Personal Notes/Action Steps:

- 9 -

IT HAPPENS

Trudy is a 15-year-old teenager with long beautiful hair who sits in an International House of Pancakes (IHOP) booth next to her mom, Kathy. The restaurant is packed with patrons on a busy Saturday morning right before Thanksgiving.

Trudy's parents are divorced. Three weeks before the interview, Trudy came back to live with her mother after spending ten months living with her father.

The 15 year old looks like a normal teenager who could easily be a high school homecoming queen or head cheerleader. At this moment in her life, Trudy is busy pushing a single order of hash browns around on her plate, awaiting the arrival of catsup. Her mom tells me she cannot eat hash browns without catsup. Trudy tells me she cannot even take a single bite before receiving the condiment. We all wait for the catsup.

After it arrives, Trudy begins eating. Together Kathy and Trudy tell me their story.

Trudy is the first to tell you she battles cystic fibrosis (CF) on a daily basis. The disease "has to do with your lungs and pancreas," she explains. With the exception of the end of an intravenous needle placement poking through her bandaged forearm, Trudy appears the picture of perfect health. Such is not the case.

Trudy was first diagnosed with cystic fibrosis at age eight weeks. One in every 3,900 babies in the United States is born with cystic fibrosis, considered one of the most common fatal genetic disorders in the country. Approximately 30,000 American children and young adults have cystic fibrosis. The disease is an incurable hereditary disorder in which the body secretes abnormally thick, sticky mucus that clogs the pancreas and the lungs. This secretion leads to breathing and digestive problems, infection, and untimely death.

Thirty years ago cystic fibrosis killed most babies before they reached early childhood. Despite medical advancements, the disease remains incurable. However, the long-term outlook has improved over time. Now more than 60 percent of babies born with the disease reach adulthood. The journey, however, is not without hardships and struggles.

When Trudy was six weeks old, she became ill with respiratory syncytial virus (RSV) infection, a normally non-alarming virus that attacks the respiratory tract, the mouth, nose, eyes, throat, and lungs. Although the illness is relatively common in both children and adults, Trudy's symptoms were serious enough that she was admitted to the hospital for several days. A few days after she was released, the symptoms returned.

Trudy's pediatrician knew something was wrong, especially given the fact that she was always breathing heavily and frequently vomited right after eating. At age six weeks she was referred to a pulmonary specialist.

Confirming a cystic fibrosis diagnosis with certainty involves conducting a sweat test. Sweat tests measure the amount of salt in a person's body. Kathy remembers the day well.

"They wanted to sweat test Trudy just to make sure that it wasn't CF. The physician knew something was wrong because of the weight gain despite the vomiting, the RSV. But she didn't, of course, suspect CF," Trudy's mom recalls.

"They did a sweat test on her, which was like a watch, a little watch they put on her arm. And it gathered sweat. CF patients have high doses of sodium in their system. It was like a 20-minute test. Then we had the results later that day," she says. "After the physician got the positive back on the test, they called us back in, and they told her father and me. They said that she had CF because she had a high dose of sodium in her system."

Kathy vividly remembers being told that Trudy's life span would be limited because of CF. "The physician had told us at that time that they expected the life span to be under 20 years. Because ten years before that, it wasn't more than childhood," she states. "It took a while for the information to soak in. The pulmonary specialist immediately hospitalized Trudy and kept her for about a week. And they treated her for her symptoms. All they could do at that time was treat the symptoms, you know, get the mucus out of her lungs."

"At that time, we started on a regimen of nebulized (breathing) treatments and patting her body at different places two or three times a day (much like is done on the backs of babies needing to burp) to clear out the mucus in her lungs." Kathy begins patting Trudy in various places on her body to show me the ritual she has done since Trudy was six months old.

At this point in the interview, Trudy finishes her hash browns. I ask Kathy when exactly she told Trudy she had cystic fibrosis. She replies quickly: "She always knew."

"How is that?" I ask.

"Because we had a son, two years older than her, so there was another child who didn't have all of that." Trudy does not disagree with her mother's assessment.

Even as the patting and medical treatments for Trudy continued, her growing-up time was relatively normal with certain exceptions. During her eighth and ninth grades, she was homebound for a majority of the time because of her illness.

Trudy is a good student and seems to enjoy going to school. When asked what school is like for her in the midst of periodic hospital visits and routinely needing to be patted, Trudy replies, "It's—I don't know how to explain it. It's just something that I've always done. It's not bad, sometimes it is—sometimes it's bad. But, I have to do it, so . . . ."

Trudy prefers not to dwell on her illness. Kathy believes the family has talked less about the illness, as opposed to simply taking it as an "everyday occur-rence." As medical advancements have been made over time, Trudy's expected life span has increased from 20 to 30 years.

"I just try not to think about it. If I dwell on it, I will probably make the situation worse. So I just try not to think about it," Trudy states. She says she talks to only one friend about her illness, and that is her best friend, Michele, who lives on her street. They have lunch together every two or three days. Michele is the person whom Trudy called the night before she returned to the hospital on her last visit because she was "pissed off, sad, depressed, all of it," Trudy says.

During her eighth and ninth grades, Trudy's body began to give way to the cystic fibrosis. As Trudy and her mom remember, the 15 year old began a slow death march while she waited for a must-have transplant in order to live.

The 14 months of waiting were incredibly hard on the 15 year old and her family. At times Trudy was uncertain as to whether she wanted to live or die.

"For awhile there, I didn't care. It didn't feel like I was ready for a transplant. The first time that we got the call that lungs had been found for me, I wasn't ready at all. I didn't want to go through the surgery. I wasn't physically, emotionally ready," Trudy explains.

Perhaps Trudy's reticence was visionary. As the situation unfolded, the lungs initially found for Trudy were not medically appropriate for her. A similar situation happened a second time, again after the family rushed Trudy to a large metropolitan hospital for another potential transplant.

As the saying goes, the third time worked like a charm. After spending an afternoon talking with hospice chaplains and praying to God, Kathy received a call that once again a new set of lungs had become available that might work for Trudy.

"We had talked that afternoon, and we had prayed and everything, and sure enough, we got the call that night," Kathy says. For the third time Trudy's parents rushed her to the hospital. This time the lung transplantation was successful.

When asked how that makes her feel, Trudy says she feels both happy and sad.

"I can do a lot more. I can do a lot more running than I used to be able to," she says.

Even though she may miss school from time to time, Trudy is required daily to work with a computer for medical purposes. Using a laptop, Trudy takes a deep breath and blows into a mouthpiece that has a sensor connected to the computer. Looking at the screen, Trudy can immediately see the lines from her breathing that measure her lung capacity.

The numbers from the breathing test that Trudy is looking for on the computer screen range from 105 and 115, acceptable and usual numbers for her. If the numbers are bad, Trudy knows to immediately call her physician.

Prior to her most recent hospital stay just before the interview, her numbers dropped to 70 and then even lower because of a cold. Even a common cold can be deadly for individuals with CF like Trudy.

Talking about Trudy's illness within her family unit is complicated. Both of her parents have remarried. They converse together and share in the responsibility of caring for Trudy. Both sets of parents are capable of handling her intravenous fluid (IV) and medication needs at home as warranted.

"We just transported her from house to house. I guess we ran a portable hospital out of the house," Kathy says.

Over the years the entire family has undergone psychological therapy in a variety of ways to try to better cope with Trudy's situation in addition to the challenges of simple, everyday living within blended families. Therapy seems to have helped.

"We talked about the fact that she was dying because she was. I think the fact that we had a therapist for a year and a half or two years is the only reason the five of us got through it," Kathy says. "The therapist helped the four adults do a lot. And I highly recommend a non-partial therapist for the child and then for the adults."

Like most teenagers, Trudy is looking forward to her future independence. She is excited about getting her driver's license when she turns 16. When she begins dating, she plans on talking with her boyfriends about her illness, but she wants to avoid making a big deal of the matter.

"It's hard to tell, but eventually the illness just comes out. I'm scared of rejection," Trudy says.

In the meantime, the 15 year old and her mother seem to experience tension when talking about who is in control of Trudy's health care decisions. Trudy suggests that "no matter what," her physician decides her course of treatment now. Her mom chimes in quickly: "her father and I decide the course of treatment with her physician."

Parent-child relationships are challenging in the best of times. For young people with CF like Trudy, perhaps the stark reality of living with the disease can make parental relationships even more complicated for numerous reasons, including the fact that the disease itself is handed down to children from parents.

For whatever the real reasons, things seem strained between Trudy and Kathy at times during the interview. How much of their tension stemmed from Trudy's illness as opposed to usual teenage daughter challenges is unknown.

Yet tensions are evidenced during several points of the interview, as would be expected. Although she is seated next to her mom, she tells me, "I'm closer to my dad; I'm a daddy's girl so I'm closer to my dad. But I have to talk to my mom, too." She also comments that regardless of her relationships with her parents, "it always comes down to my best friend, Michelle."

"Her whole entire life, she's lived with me. She's only lived with her dad these last ten months. But she's still a daddy's girl. But that's okay," Kathy says.

Germs are a constant worry for individuals like Trudy who live with life-threatening diseases. Many children and young people battling serious illnesses in pediatric hospitals are seen wearing masks as they walk around the units pushing IV hanging bags on steel carriers.

While Trudy was living with her father, she met another young girl with cystic fibrosis but was unable to talk with her because of the worry of spreading germs between them.

"She could have some bacteria that she could give me. I could have some bacteria that I could give her," Trudy explains.

"They could talk if they sat four feet away from each other. But I don't think either of them made the attempt," her mother says. Handshakes can also be problematic and are to be avoided, according to Kathy and Trudy.

Although Trudy identifies her friend Michele as her closest confidant in talking about her illness, she does at times reach out to her 18-year-old brother. In fact, she seems genuinely happy and surprised that her brother recently visited her in the hospital with a friend of his.

"He came up and saw me the other day before I left the hospital, which is unusual. He doesn't like hospitals too much. It shocked me," Trudy says.

When asked if Trudy ever wonders why she has CF and her brother does not, she replies:

"I've asked him that before."

"And his response?" I ask.

"He just says, 'it happens.'" She shrugs.

Trudy readily admits to becoming jaded while battling CF her entire lifetime. The situation has changed over time, depending on her age and emotional state.

"The first time that I ever went into the hospital, I was seven and I hated it then. When I was 12, I went in and I was all happy because I was missing school. And then I got older and felt jaded; too much was going on in my life."

When asked if she views her life as short, medium, or long, she replies, "I don't look at it that way. I just do what I do. What I can do. With my friends."

Medical scientists point to cystic fibrosis as one of the more promising areas of research in modern medicine. On a personal note, Trudy and her mom are continuing to pursue any and all available opportunities for new knowledge.

After finishing the conversation at the IHOP, they will drive to a larger city to attend a seminar on cystic fibrosis being led by Trudy's primary physician. Kathy uses such support group educational sessions as ways to "pick up what other parents are going through," she says. "You give them suggestions on things that you went through because there are a lot of new patients with small babies. And you can tell them things that we remember when our children were small."

On a daily basis, Trudy and Kathy continue to move through their lives, viewing the challenge presented by cystic fibrosis as an "everyday occurrence," Kathy says. "We're just like a normal household."

Whether she lives for a few more years until she is 20 or 30, or defies the odds and lives much longer, Trudy sees her life as a composite of mixed blessings and future uncertainties. She prefers not to talk about her illness and does not care what words other people use when they do. She oftentimes seems especially frustrated over being sick. She fondly remembers her years before her lung transplant as "having a good life." She continues to pray to God "just for health," she explains.

For now, Trudy seems grateful to be a "normal" teenager who just happens to have another person's lungs in her body, although at times she is sad as a result of the transplant. She recommends that other cystic fibrosis patients "do the treatment as much as they can because even though it may seem like something really good, to get new lungs, it's not really all that good." In the next few days Trudy hopes to begin feeling better soon to avoid another hospital stay like the one she just completed because of a cold.

The future for Trudy is uncertain. Her transplanted lungs are expected to last around five or ten years. At that time she can ask to receive another set of lungs if she desires. In the meantime, regardless of how normal her life may be or appear, she thinks about the future in a unique way.

"I just wonder how long the lungs are going to last," she ponders.

Epilogue

In 2008, Trudy continues to do well and is presently in her second year of college. Her mother says Trudy does anything and everything humanly possible.

It Happens
An Interviewer's Perspective

A Lesson Learned – *Balancing*

Trudy and her mom were balancing a lot on their plates. During the best of times, running a household with teenagers is no easy task. Yet Kathy was facing each day head-on and asking for help from therapists and medical experts and others along the way. Trudy was doing much the same in her own way. "I just do what I do. What I can do," Trudy explained.

Indeed, as former Beatle John Lennon is quoted as saying, "life is what happens when you're busy making other plans." In order to deal with life, including a life in which a teenager is chronically ill, *balancing* becomes ever important, as Trudy and Kathy each mentioned in their own ways.

Just do what you can do, *balancing* along the way. And don't beat yourself up if the journey isn't perfect or pretty.

Suggested Response Strategies/Discussion Questions/ Commentary:

** If you know of a family struggling with a serious illness of one of the members, don't forget to inquire about all of the members of the family and not just the one ill person. This is especially true when young people are involved.

** Think about how you are taking care of yourself as you take care of others. Are you getting enough rest in order to help those who cannot sleep? If you are encouraging your sick loved one to try to eat something, are you yourself eating something healthy at least once a day?

** Evaluate if you are delegating enough or asking for help in order to keep things balanced and on an even keel, to the extent possible. Make changes when necessary.

** Let go of the notion that things must be perfect or orderly. Now is not the time to watch television shows where everyone's house is spotless, gourmet meals are being prepared, everyone is communicating well, and life is fine.

** Get some fresh air every single day. If you are maintaining a hospital or bedside vigil, set up a system in which you can step outside for a few minutes to take a quick walk.

Your Personal Notes/Action Steps:

BLISTERED

Today is a good day for 15-year-old Oscar because he is "not tired or anything," he says. Oscar is a stoic young man who responds in short answers and uses the word "yeah" a great deal. He just spent Thanksgiving week in the hospital.

In one ear Oscar is wearing a shiny jewel given to him by his dad. His father and mother are sitting on each side of him in his small hospital room. Oscar is one of 15 children. His dad is sitting in a wheelchair for lack of another regular chair, and his mother sits in a straight chair. I sit down on a physician's stool that has a tendency to roll. Oscar watches out for the tape recorder so that it does not fall. Doctors and nurses come in and out of the colorless hospital room almost one right after the other. The scenario is chaotic at best.

On this particular hospital visit, Oscar has a roommate a few feet away—a tiny baby girl receiving chemotherapy through intravenous bags hanging on a short little roller. The baby is wearing a large pink bow around her balding head. The bow gives the room the only bright color visible. Otherwise things are stainless and black and gray.

The day before, this same little baby with the same bow on her head was sitting at the nurses' station in her stroller. Her short IV hanging-bag stand was next to her. She was laughing and giggling and holding court with all the nurses.

Today things have changed for the baby. She hollers loudly; evidently nothing is wrong with her lungs. She fusses and frets constantly. With a chronically pained expression, her mother does a variety of things to try to comfort her baby as the baby jerks about on her mother's lap. Her mother tries to hold her tight, being ever mindful that the baby's intravenous drip must remain stable. Nothing seems to help this little one on this particular day. As Baby Bow Girl continues to fuss, Oscar and his parents tell me about their lives.

Murphy's Law suggests anything that can go wrong, will go wrong. Such is the case for Oscar. Although he has been coming to the hospital for chemotherapy treatment for over ten years, Oscar is getting progressively worse. In 1994 he was first diagnosed with acute lymphocytic leukemia (ALL), a cancer of the blood. Since that time, his condition has deteriorated. Just recently he relapsed with brain cancer. He will continue with additional chemotherapy treatments for the time being.

Under pressure, things get worse. So suggests Murphy's Law of Thermodynamics.

There is not a moment that passes in any of these interviews in which I am not overwhelmed by the perseverance and attitudes of those who are sharing their stories. This is true for Oscar and his parents. This family is struggling mightily. Perhaps they have always struggled. Before the actual interview begins and the tape recorder is turned on, Oscar is asked to go down the hall for a brief procedure. His mother goes with him. I remain in the hospital room with Oscar's father as the baby continues to holler.

The first five years of Oscar's life were "normal." The next ten years have been anything but, given the amount of time he has spent in and out of hospitals battling leukemia and now brain cancer. Oscar is incredibly astute in knowing the specific details of his medical treatments, including what his statistical numbers and counts mean in terms of future treatments.

When asked how he feels to have spent over ten years battling cancer, he responds, "I've been here so many times, I'm used to it."

Although Oscar does not talk very much in general, he believes hearing what his nurses have to say about his condition is helpful because then he knows what is coming his way. Although he has been coming to the hospital for years, battling brain cancer is different in some ways than battling leukemia. Oscar is especially appreciative of the physicians and nurses who ask him what he wants. Not only do they ask him if he needs anything in the way of physical items such as water or a blanket, they also ask him how he wants to hear the latest news involving his condition.

"They ask me first if I want them to tell me straight out." He prefers "regular, straight-out words," but does not elaborate.

Anticipation is challenging. Knowledge makes things easier. For now, as always, the family will take things one day at a time. Oscar's father speaks at great length about his own ongoing frustration over his son's situation, including the inconveniences of receiving medical care away from home.

"Oscar never talks to me about his illness," he says. "Him and I never talk about it, and I don't know if Mom does or not."

Oscar's father talks more during the interview than either Oscar or his mom. Both Oscar's mother and father remember their son's initial diagnosis of leukemia in 1993 when Oscar had barely started school at age five. His mother comments: "I remember my own mother saying, 'You know, this doesn't look right, this doesn't look right.' I guess she was telling me because she at that time wasn't working full time, and I guess she was seeing television shows about diseases or something like that," she adds. "And then I went to work and my husband went to work, and then he came back from what I remember, and he took Oscar to the physician and found out what he had. And then he went to my job to let me know so we could tell Oscar."

Oscar's father recalls, "I took Oscar to school that morning to tell them that I was going to pick him up at 10 o'clock because if they are in school until 10, they are accounted for the whole day. I was told somebody from Child Protective Services wanted to talk to me because of Oscar's bruises. I told the lady, 'Well, that's why I'm taking him to the doctor. Well, you don't think I'm hurting my son, do you?' And she said, 'Well, we need to make sure.' And I said, 'Well, he's my only son, I wouldn't do that.'

"Well, she answered loudly and she said, 'Sometimes parents single them out.' And I'm like *I don't need this.* So when she turned her back, we took off, and I took him to the doctor," he recalls. Then he turned to his son and asks, "Do you remember?" Oscar did not respond.

Oscar's mother explains that her son's severe bruising had started the week before his initial diagnosis.

"Then it was finally when we came home, and we saw him on top of the fence by the tree, remember? He said that he had fallen and hurt himself. And that's where I thought the black eyes had come from. And it wasn't even from that," she says.

When the initial diagnosis was made, the physician first asked Oscar's parents if they would go into his office to sit down and talk.

"I said '*no*, you need to tell me right now where we stand,' " Oscar's father remembers demanding. The physician told them that Oscar had leukemia. The family went straight to the pediatric cancer hospital.

Murphy's Constant suggests that matter will be damaged in direct proportion to its value. Like all families, Oscar and his family are damaged, yet to a greater degree because of their life realities. Experts suggest receiving a terminal diagnosis can be likened to the effect of looking directly at the sun: "it blinds, it is intense, and it can cause damage."[3]

For Oscar and his parents, this is the second time in their lives they are looking directly at the sun. Leukemia first, now brain cancer. They are hurting in their own ways. Oscar's mom said she will maintain her vigil in "faith and trust" and will continue to "pray for the people who are helping you. Give them knowledge and wisdom. That God may, you know, that the hands may be His hands as far as the healing and the care."

Listening to this family's conversation is a challenge. These individuals struggle with each other much of the time. Yet no doubt the parents both love their son. Perhaps leaving the room as Oscar's mother did for much of the interview is a way to keep the peace or minimize the discord during these tough times.

For me personally, I imagine a great deal of anger and pain on the part of 15-year-old Oscar who has leukemia and is now facing brain cancer. Because Oscar has refused to say very much in front of his parents, I can only imagine his internal thoughts when he hears his father complain about his own health care and having to drive 28 miles to the hospital to see his son, all the while trying to convince his son that he knows exactly what the younger boy is experiencing and feeling.

For Oscar and his family, there is a strong sense based on both conversation and observance that Murphy's Laws are wearing them down. They are tired and weary after ten years of fighting on a variety of fronts. Yet for whatever their reasons, they have shared part of their afternoon and their stories with a total stranger.

Within the nucleus of the family unit, a 15-year-old boy whose future remains highly marginalized imagines a better and more hopeful world for others like him. As I ask Oscar one of the final questions of the interview, it is one of the few times in the conversation that he does not shrug and say "yeah" or "nah" or nothing at all.

"What would you say to other newly diagnosed cancer patients your age?"

He deliberately takes hold of a silver necklace with a cross on it from underneath his shirt and responds, "Everything will be all right."

Epilogue

As his physical predicament grew worse, Oscar decided to stop going to the hospital for chemotherapy treatments. His physician said the decision was against his parents' wishes. The stoic young man with the shiny earring and silver cross necklace died in the early part of 2004.

Blistered
An Interviewer's Perspective

A Lesson Learned - *Disbanding*

The story "Blistered" is entitled as such because so many old wounds seemed to be festering within this family, at least from my brief conversation with Oscar and his parents. Oscar was struggling with his dad; his mom and dad were significantly struggling with each other. All of this tension made the reality of Oscar's illness more difficult for everyone, especially for Oscar, who was at the heart of the cross fire.

Perhaps within family units there is a benefit to *disbanding* old negative and harmful ways of interacting with family members when someone becomes seriously ill. This, of course, is easier written and said than done. Yet perhaps when someone becomes seriously ill, especially a young person, a neon sign can go off in our minds and psyches that we need to disband our armor and lay down some of our old, long-standing inabilities to get along. At least it's worth a shot.

Suggested Response Strategies/Discussion Questions/ Commentary:

** After an initial diagnosis of a life-threatening illness, bring the immediate family unit together for a serious conversation about how the family is going to collectively face the illness. Consider involving a neutral third party to help guide that conversation as the situation allows, e.g. a clergy person or trusted friend or therapist. Try to agree to set aside old issues, problems, ways of interacting (or not interacting) with each other. Agree to the minimum specifics of a plan for moving forward. If people simply cannot get along, decide on when hospital or medical visits will take place, where and with whom. Consider involving hospice personnel or other medical professionals in those visits. Social workers or counselors can also be extremely helpful.

Your Personal Notes/Action Steps:

-11-

GOOD NEWS, *MIJITO*! WHAT THE HELL!

Frequently there are great moments and days in a children's cancer hospital, like when good news is delivered to a patient. On this particular day, 16-year-old Arthur is doing wheelies in his wheelchair in a hospital room, having just received some good news: his blood counts are doing fine, and "there is no trace of leukemia anymore," his mother, Iris, says. Iris is grinning from ear to ear when she says those words.

Arthur is anxious to tell his story about when he first learned he had leukemia in 2001 and about his life up until that day when he received his good news. Even though the hour is late, and the mother and son have a three-hour drive ahead of them, both are willing to stay in order to be interviewed. Arthur is also grinning from ear to ear as he continues to circle around the center of his little hospital room in his wheelchair.

Arthur's mother talks a lot, which seems to frustrate the 16 year old. Arthur wants to tell his own story, his way. He perseveres.

Throughout the dialogue, the give and take between Arthur and his mom is consistently funny and poignant. Iris is a happy-go-lucky large woman with an ample bosom. She switches from English to Spanish and

155

back again in the blink of an eye. One immediately senses that she is without hesitation the ringleader and matriarch of her family, for whom the saying was written: "Mama ain't happy? Nobody's happy." Iris repeatedly referred to her son in loving terms of endearment in Spanish, such as *mijito* (my son).

While Arthur and his mother play point/counterpoint, I feel as if I am watching a tennis volley or television episode of *Everybody Loves Raymond* in which Raymond's meddlesome and martyr mother, Marie, is bugging her fully-grown sons. Marie is telling them what to say and when, interrupting them when they try to say what she's told them to say, then re-explaining what they said because they said it all wrong. Marie even periodically pinches her boys on their cheeks and makes kissy-faces with them, to which they finally explode in total uniform exasperation, "MAAAAAA!" Iris could be Marie. Arthur could be a young Raymond.

Much is the same within this mother-son relationship. In fact, Iris even looks like Marie. Because of all the motherly interruptions, at times I think Arthur is simply going to rear back and ram his wheelchair right into his mother's chair to get her to hush.

An example of one of many exchanges between the 15 year old and his mom:

Interviewer: (to Arthur) "Do you remember when they first told you about the leukemia?"

(Arthur begins to answer. His mother immediately interrupts.)

Iris (mother): "We all went to pick him up from school and that's when he saw us, and then all of us went to the doctor's office. All of us entered the doctor's office. And they were ready for us with a room and everything, and I said 'Oh my God, what's happening?' But then we came into the room, and we sat down, and he was on the table, right—the examining table? And then the doctor came in. And then, Arthur, what did the doctor say?"

Arthur: "You're telling the whole story."

(He looks frustrated at his mother.)

Iris: "No, please." (She sits back in her chair, pouts, and puts her purse on her lap. She motions for her son to speak.)

Arthur (to his mother): "Say what you want to say."

Iris: "Well, that's all I wanted to say."

Iris then stoically looks away with no animation for the next few seconds, as if she is mad and is not going to say another word whatsoever. Within less than a few minutes, however, she becomes animated again and interrupts her son. Another conversation just like the above takes place. This type of exchange happens over and over throughout the interview.

Nosebleeds were among several indications that something was wrong with Arthur. One day when he was nearly 15, he recalls feeling especially poorly. He had awakened with a nosebleed and was dizzy.

"I woke up, and I went to get a glass of water, and I was walking," he recalls. "I felt real dizzy, and I hit the wall on the side of the garage. I spilled the water, and was like, 'Oh shit.'"

With that, his mother quickly interrupts and tells her son, "Don't say bad words."

"Well, that's what I said," he replies. Iris glares at her son.

During this early point in the interview, I explain to both of them that total honesty in remembering the way things truly happened and what was said is preferred. I also try to reassure them that their actual names will not be used in any final documents. Iris continues to glare at her son and act embarrassed.

Despite feeling badly, Arthur went on to school at Iris' insistence because he already had too many absences.

"I didn't want you to miss too many days. They were saying he had too many absences," Iris explains. "But before that happened, I had already took him to the hospital . . . to see the family practitioner. . . . She did some lab work, and then she called me and said: 'Oh, you know what? He needs something else, um, I remember exactly. He needs CA 125. That's the name of the lab work, CA 125.' But CA means cancer. I was a medical office assistant. I did recall that the CA test was for cancer, and that's what she said." While Iris was talking with the physician and nurse, Arthur was at school continuing to have a particularly rough morning.

"I had like first period, and it was reading," Arthur says. "I had a reading class, and I told my teacher that I wasn't feeling too good, and she said that I looked pale. I went to the nurse and I told her, 'Hey, I feel bad.' And she said, 'Oh yeah, you look real bad, you look pale.'

"Second period class I was there, and they called me on the intercom that I was going home, and I was like, cool, okay. And then I went to the office.

"I was just waiting there, and my mom, it took her like ten minutes to get there. She came in, and she signed something, and it was like, well . . ." Arthur hesitated before saying what he wanted to say. Then he spoke and said what he thought to himself at the time: "What the f---?' I say 'What the f---?"

Now Oscar's mother looks as if she is going to have a heart attack. I say nothing. Iris shoots her son another look and pleads with him, *"Mijito,* please." Arthur continues, "and I thought someone had died because of the way she was . . . and we were all. I got into the truck, and we were on the way to the clinic, and it was all serious."

Together the family made the three-hour drive to a nearby metropolitan area. The medical staff was waiting for Arthur.

"We're in this room, and then I sat down on this table where they do all this stuff. And the doctor sat down and he said, 'Your son, *tu hijo tiene leucemia.'*

"And all of a sudden my dad just started crying and got very freaked out, and I got freaked out," Arthur remembers.

"I was like, what the hell, what is that? And my father was crying for like five minutes or something, and we were all quiet. My brother was just like quiet and my mother was like, 'Stop it, you are going to make Arthur cry. You are scaring him.' And the doctor was like, 'Okay, cry it out,'" Arthur recalls. "I said, 'okay doctor, what is *que es lucemia?'* And he said *'es cancer en tu sangre.'* And I'm like 'it's cancer in my blood?' Oh, what the shit? Me? Cancer? What the hell." Arthur specifically remembers hearing the word leukemia for the first time.

"I didn't know leukemia. I didn't know that word," Arthur says. "But I did know what cancer meant. Cancer is like for old people. I'm not old, what the hell," he reflects. The immediacy and severity of the situation was not lost on the 14 year old.

"They said, 'Okay, you guys are supposed to, I've already called the doctors over there, and you have to go to the cancer clinic (in the larger hospital) right now. Don't even go home and pack, right now, real serious, just drive over there.' And then we went and we were driving on the way, and then my dad and everyone was all crying, and my mom, she was all nervous. I don't know what she was thinking," he recalls. Then he turns to his mom and asks her, "What were you thinking?" The exchange seems to indicate they have never relived that moment in terms of learning what the other person was experiencing.

Iris' mind was racing at the time. "Everybody was crying. My husband was crying the two hours, three hours, in the back of the car, the truck, he was with Arthur and hugging him and crying and crying and crying and crying. And I was like, oh my God," Iris recalls.

"I'm always too hungry, because I always like to eat too much back then," she jokes and laughs, inferring that she does not eat too much now. "No, but anyway, I was not even hungry. I didn't even want to eat on the way. We stopped to get some hamburgers on the way, but we just ordered some Diet Cokes or whatever. But we were not able to eat, because we were not hungry." The family raced to the large pediatric hospital during which time Iris hoped and prayed for a good doctor.

"And I said, 'oh my God, I hope that we find a good doctor.' We didn't expect nothing, we did not know too much about leukemia. Arthur knows what cancer is. I know cancer. Cancer of the lungs, or whatever. But to me, I didn't know what was involved with leukemia to the extent that I do now," Iris recalls.

"So when we got here, they do the spinal tap right away, and they said that he didn't have any leukemia in the spinal tap, but that the white blood cell count was very high. It was 300,000. The normal is 5,000 to 10,000 white blood cells, and he had 300,000 so it was very high—at risk. So they gave him very aggressive treatment to cure the leukemia, and that's what they would do," she adds.

The family stayed at the large cancer hospital for a month during their initial visit. The weeks were hard, especially when Arthur hallucinated because of the chemotherapy and steroids.

His mother begins: "One time in the middle of the night ..." Arthur interrupts her seemingly because it is his story to tell.

"There was this one time that I woke up, like, I had a dream that I was going to kill everybody on earth but, like, with my eye, like Cyclops, kind of like XMEN. But like if I opened my eyes, I would kill everything," he remembers. "And I woke up screaming and I was like, oh wow."

There were other episodes as well in the midst of never-ending vomiting. Arthur recalls another time when he was back at home in his own bed:

"I woke up, and I thought I was dead. I was. I woke up, and I still thought I was dreaming. But it was real. I was just in my bed. I was like, 'Oh, what am I doing, is this where I'm supposed to be?' And like, I'm dead. What am I doing here? I know I'm in my room, but it's not my room. And I was like, getting up, and moving around and trying to know where I am," he adds.

His mom quickly interjects, "It was terrible."

Arthur continues. "I was like, what the hell? And then I looked out the window, and I was like, I'm still here, but I'm not here. I was banging on my door and saying 'Help me, someone help me.' I just got on my bed and made myself into a ball and was like, what the hell, what the hell? I remembered, hey, well, open the door. And if I remembered and if it opened, I would be alive. And so I opened the door and I was like, oh, okay. Then I went to my mom's room and my dad's room, and I was like that night I was all scared."

Iris quickly interjects, "Yeah, he was all scared."

When he was first diagnosed two years ago, Arthur wondered every day what was going to happen to him. He wondered about his treatments, where he would spend his time, how sick he would be, and so on.

Over time Arthur has become less concerned about his daily issues and more philosophical. He appreciates the help of the medical staff in that they "make you feel comfortable in knowing what's going to happen to you. And they make you more open-minded about what's going on. They prepare you for what's coming next," he adds.

When asked what he thinks about now in terms of his life, he replies, "Uh, I don't know, thank God I'm alive."

Arthur is practical in his thinking about how young people should be told they have cancer. "Well, now, I think there is no other way (than straightforward) to tell you that you have cancer because I mean, because you think at that time, oh gee, 12 years old, real harsh, could you tell me in a nicer way? How well or nice can it be told? 'Gee, hee hee, you've got cancer,' or like, 'you've got cancer.' I mean, 'you've got cancer.'" (Arthur uses a variety of voice inflections here).

This 16-year-old straight-talker continues to be practical and bodacious, much to his mother's chagrin at times.

"If you just have cancer, there is nothing else they can do. Like, you're paralyzed, what do you do, you go to the doctor, 'Gee doc, I'm paralyzed, what do you got for me? Why don't you take this wheelchair and roll your ass around town.' And like blind people, 'Oh, I'm blind, oh I'm blind, what do you got for me? Why don't you take this dog and let him drag your ass around. I mean, what the hell? If you just got shit, there is nothing else. There is nothing else you can do," Arthur comments. His mother continues to glare at her son.

Arthur has been told twice that he has cancer. He relapsed after his initial diagnosis. This time the cancer was found in his spine. His physician called his mother on a Friday afternoon.

"The doctor called me . . . on Friday to let me know that something was wrong," Iris recalls. Then he called her back because he was aware of the difficult weekend she would have if she did not know what was wrong, so he told her by phone.

"'I want to tell you by phone, but I want to see you on Monday.' And he told me Arthur got leukemia again on his spine. The spinal tap is where they saw the little traces of leukemia. So he told me it's just a little," Iris explains. "I told the doctor, 'Okay, but don't tell Arthur.' I didn't want to tell anyone, because I didn't want to."

Arthur recalls: "I came in first this time, and the medical team members came in. They wanted to talk to my parents first. I waited in the room, and I was watching

TV, and they called me, 'Hey, come in here.' The doctor was sitting down, and Dad, Mom, and the nurses (whom he called by name). My nurse was there, and she was like kind of crying. Well, like, tears in her eyes. And I was like, oh shit. 'Straight up,'" Arthur told them. Arthur's physician spoke to him.

"'Arthur, you have cancer again. We found some in your spine, and it's going to your head. You have cancer again,' he stated." Arthur says that his doctor was visibly upset when he delivered the news.

"Oh yeah. He was kind of like, watery eyes, and my dad had watery eyes, and he said, 'The only thing we can do is just do a bone marrow transplant. I don't want you to think that everything we have been doing with the chemotherapy is just a total waste of time. It didn't work, but if you want to do the transplant so you can live . . .,' and I said, 'Well, yeah. Do it. I want to live. Do this,' " Arthur demanded.

Arthur's big brother was his bone marrow donor. "My brother and me, well, I love him to death because he's my big brother, and he always takes care of me," Arthur explains.

At one point Arthur's older brother told him, "You know, I'm always there for you and thank God that you and I have the same blood for you to be alive." Arthur calls such conversations "brotherish."

Not only is Arthur extremely close to his brother, he speaks very fondly of his father. Trading places with his son is something Arthur's dad wishes he could do, according to the 16 year old.

"Sometimes with my dad, he's just quiet about it. He doesn't want to show how he feels, but I know how he feels. He doesn't want me suffering. He would rather want himself to suffer than to see me suffer. It hurts to see me in pain," he adds.

All of the family members think about the possibility of Arthur's death from cancer. The reality that in the last two years cancer has been found in his blood, spine, and brain is especially discouraging.

"Yeah, everyone thinks about death," Arthur says. Yet he is philosophical and seemingly resolved in his words: "If the day comes, there's no stopping it," he states matter-of-factly. In the meantime, Arthur is optimistic.

"I've always thought about going on. . . . 'Oh, I have cancer again' (simulating a conversation in reference to his last relapse). It's not going to stop me. I'll keep on going forever." He continues with a question that he answers himself: "Why don't I give up? I want to live, all to the fullest in this life, before I go to the next."

For Iris, things seem to be not quite as simple or straightforward. Perhaps she talks and interrupts her son a lot to sort things out in her own mind or to make things better for her son. Whatever the reason, Iris readily admits she is scared about the possibility of Arthur dying.

"I'm scared about him dying for sure. I always thought that I'm not going to make it if he dies. I don't know what I'm going to do. But God has given me strength to focus. My faith is that he is going to survive, because God already made a miracle on his life. I know it for sure, and when God makes a miracle, He doesn't take it away. He gives you the miracle and that's it.

"And I know that I have two sons only, and through my oldest son he gave me the life of this one (looking at her son sitting in the wheelchair), because of his blood that he gave to him. So I try not to think of that. But when I was thinking, one time he was very sick, like two or three times he was very sick here in the hospital, so I was crying too much, because I don't want for him to be dead. I don't want to, and I know that my husband is not going to tolerate my constant crying—nobody is going to tolerate that, but I just keep on praying and praying and praying every day.

"I'm happy now. I'm happier than before because I know that he is doing good, even though he is not walking this moment, but he's here, and he's going to walk; this is not forever. This is just for his bones to get better. So I'm trying not to think that something bad is going to happen to him because I know that he's okay," she adds.

Regardless of what may or may not be in store for him in the future, Arthur continues to understand that others are in similar and oftentimes worse medical situations. When he first saw young children who had lost legs to cancer, the 14 year old told Iris, "Oh, Mom, you see, I should be happy. I'm happy at least I have all my legs and arms. At least I have only leukemia. At least I don't have cancer in my legs, Mom, because look, it's better than them. I have leukemia, and I am better than them that have cancer in their legs because they don't have legs. At least me, I can walk."

Yet his mother oftentimes sees things differently than her son, including when her son said he was glad he did not have bone cancer.

"I said to myself (although she is now saying this in front of her son), it's worse for you *mijito*, because you have cancer in your whole blood. Imagine that. But I'm not going to take away that illusion that it's better to have leukemia than cancer of the legs. But I'm not going to take away what you were thinking. To you, it was doing you good," she said to her son. "Because if I said, 'it's worse, *mijito*, because of' " . . . Her voice trails off. She does not finish her sentence.

What sustains Iris is her love for her family and her faith. If she were talking to a new parent of a child with cancer, she would tell him or her: "It doesn't matter what the doctor tells you, you have to believe in what Jesus says. That God says that if you believe in Him, you have to walk by faith, not what you see around. If the doctor says he has cancer, it's not the end of the world. You just have to focus your life, everything on the word of Jesus, and with Jesus. Or you believe in God, you are going to make it. Because there is only so much that you can do. Yes, it's going to be difficult because you are not accustomed to your routine, and what you do in every-day life.

"It's going to change everything," she continues. "It's going to change too many things. You are going to have to be with him all the time in the hospital, and you have to worry about the temperatures coming up and down. Because if you see a hike in temperature, and you don't take care of that, then he can die."

In the last two years, Iris has spent most of her life taking care of her youngest son in addition to her work, her older son, her husband, and her extended family. She almost talks like a rock star's road manager in that she does "all the booking" for his medical appoint-ments, which she never misses for any reason.

She is also his driver, making the three-hour one-way visit to and from the cancer hospital at least three times a week. During one particularly bad episode for

Arthur, Iris made the six-hour round trip twice in one day. Regardless of the distance, she is eternally grateful for the hospital and its personnel who are helping her son.

Because of Arthur's consistent usage of curse words, despite repeated chastisements from his mother, I ask him toward the end of the interview if he were angry about his situation.

"I guess, in a way. I wish I were okay. Everyone has problems, even if they are not medical problems. People have problems with their marriage or child abuse. Of course, I'm angry, a little bit, but I have to deal with it," he replies stoically.

One of the ways Arthur deals with his anger is by talking to his friends. Some understand; many do not. Some of his friends simply say to Arthur, "Oh well, that sucks."

"And some of them try to give me advice, but they don't even make sense. It's like, what the hell are you talking about, are you stoned?" Arthur proclaims.

One of the most stupid things people say to Arthur, including one of his female friends with whom he goes to school, is that "things happen for a reason. People who don't really think, say that. Someone who thinks that quote is good . . ."

Arthur's mother interrupts and says to her son, "Sometimes I say that quote."

He immediately replies, "No, that's stupid!"

She retorts, "Well, sometimes I say it."

He again asks his mother, "Do you say 'Everything happens for a reason?' "

Iris responds: "Well, please, sometimes I say that." The exchange between the two ends, and the room is silent. After a few minutes, Arthur is again philosophical.

"People have their own beliefs. It just happens; okay, it just happens. But I didn't want to hear that. I wanted to hear, you know, that 'you can always talk to us about it' or 'I'm always here for you, whenever you need a friend, I'm here,' something like that. Not in those exact words, but something. I was supposed to hear some comforting words, not some stupid stuff. Yeah, it was like my school friend didn't even care. There are some people who understand and then some people who don't. That's what kind of makes me angry. She said the wrong thing, so okay, whatever," he states.

Arthur wonders if people distance themselves from people who are ill like him, especially young people, because they do not know what to say, or they may say something wrong or stupid.

"Yeah, some people don't know what to say. They kind of don't hang out with me as much as they used to. I think it's because it scares them, or they don't want to see their friend like that. But you have to see somebody like that. It's better that they are like that, and they are your friends. You can talk to them. It's like, cancer is not contagious, don't let them think that, I'm like, read a book. You have the Internet? Well use it," he adds.

Arthur begins once again to do more wheelies about the room, as he did periodically throughout the entire interview. There is a sense that he and his mother will continue their own banter throughout their three-hour drive home.

When asked what he might say to a newly diagnosed cancer patient, Arthur quickly responds.

"I would just tell him, I hope everything works out the best for you, and it's not easy. You have some hard times, you are going to feel like you want to die because of all the pain you feel. It hurts you so much, your soul, it really feels like too much.

"You just want to say, forget it. I want to die. But don't feel like that. Find other ways to make you feel better. Like, listen to music or talk to people about it. Stay occupied. Even when you feel bad, when you feel like, when you feel real bad, like something inside of me is biting me, or something, use your imagination. Pretend you are at the beach with girls all around you or something. Something. Escape from that. Hopefully you would be okay."

On this Good News day, Arthur continues his straight-talk philosophy as he does another wheelie. "Some things are worse," he comments. "I have cancer, but not anymore," he says with a smile and a turn.

Good News, *Mijito*! What the Hell!
An Interviewer's Perspective

A Lesson Learned – *Accepting*

"If the day comes, there's no stopping it," Arthur tells us. How right he is. No one is invincible. At some point, *accepting* is paramount to survival, if not progress.

Suggested Response Strategies/Discussion Questions/ Commentary:

** Is someone you know having a tough time dealing with the reality of a serious illness? Are there resources you can direct that person to in order to increase the level of acceptance?

** Think about joining a support group of other persons in similar situations to you. Ask members of the group how they are coping and accepting their situations at hand, if appropriate.

** Ask for help from clergy or spiritual persons in your area.

** Be clear about what information you want to receive from your healthcare providers in order to understand and better accept the situation you are facing. If something is unclear, ask again and again for a repeat of the information until you are certain you understand what is being told to you. Acceptance comes much easier with clarity.

Personal Notes/Action Steps:

-12-

Quiet Considerations

Jeanne looks like a stunningly beautiful model for a hair shampoo advertisement in a women's magazine that guarantees to improve your life by turning your long, dry, lifeless hair into a cascade of fine silk running down your back. Whatever she is doing to her hair, the product is working for her. Jeanne looks simply exquisite from head to toe as she enters a coffee shop next to a busy bookstore. She is 17 years old.

People watch her walk through the coffee shop. She seems not to notice. She appears to be a cross between Jackie Kennedy Onassis and Audrey Hepburn in her blue jeans, a T-shirt, and jacket. Her eyelashes are long and frame unique and expressive eyes that have been highlighted by a colorful, sparkly eye shadow. You can almost picture her on a Saturday afternoon at the mall with a group of her teenage girlfriends, each trying to decide what color of shiny eye shadow to buy. Jeanne carries a quiet and unassuming countenance with her beauty, which makes her even more attractive.

When we scheduled the interview on the phone, neither Jeanne nor I thought to tell each other what we looked like so that we would know how to find each other. She has arrived at the coffee shop well after our appointed time late one afternoon. Prior to that moment, I was convinced she was going to be a no-show, even though she knew I had driven several hours specifically to talk with her.

Although I am the only female sitting alone in the place with my tape recorder and notebook in front of me on a table I strategically selected in a corner area, she does not scan the room upon arrival. Nor does she even glance over my way to make any type of eye contact. Instead, she immediately selects a table in the middle of the room.

She sits down and orders nothing. She just sits with one elbow propped up on the table, her head resting on that elbow. Her body language suggests she is tired, bored, mad or maybe all of the above.

For a few minutes I continue to sit at my own table in the corner, wondering if this is indeed Jeanne. I know Jeanne is 17 years old, and this young women looks much older. Her captivating beauty, independence, and mobility are not things I had counted on since most of the interview respondents to date came with noticeable signs of their own medical issues like oxygen tanks and wheelchairs.

For a few minutes, we both just sit at our respective tables. Then I take the initiative and walk over to her table. She immediately looks up and smiles when I ask, "Are you Jeanne?" She shakes my hand loosely and apologizes for being late. She tells me she could not wake up from an afternoon nap after her school day ended. I thank her for agreeing to the interview, and she repeatedly says, "No problem."

Today at this coffee shop, Jeanne sits alone. Her father has dropped her off to meet me for our conversation. It seems as though she has viewed much of her life as being alone or at least different. After a few moments of idle chatter between the two of us, I move my notebook and tape recorder over to where she is sitting.

With the background noise of an aggravating coffee grinder and a young man periodically shouting, "Tall, mocha latte light" or some semblance thereof, Jeanne begins to tell me about her exceptional young life. It started 17 years ago as a healthy baby born on the cusp of a new year.

From across the table, Jeanne appears to be in picture-perfect health. She smiles a great deal, her teeth are shiny and white, and she seems to feel relatively well. She looks like any other average, albeit extraordinarily beautiful, teenager. When I begin to talk with her, however, I cannot help but notice that her expressive eyes periodically roll way back up into her head. The aberration was almost nonexistent in terms of being able to carry on a conversation. Yet it is significantly noticeable as one of the few physical abnormalities for this young woman.

Eye rolling is among the least of her problems, although it is one of the many offshoots of a lifetime of health care issues. When Jeanne was four, she was diagnosed with chronic myeloid leukemia (CML), a slowly progressing cancer that affects the body's white blood cells. CML is considered rare in that it affects only about 6,000 new individuals every year. Jeanne's brother was her bone marrow transplant donor.

Jeanne has been in remission from the leukemia for 13 years. Other problems have arisen, however, creating significant long-term health care issues for her.

One of her problems is that she has been diagnosed with Stevens-Johnson Syndrome (SJS), an illness causing severe swelling and destruction of the skin and mucous membranes that usually begins in the form of a body rash. Given that the mucus membranes eventually become involved with the rash, ulcerations can form on the eyelids and within the mouth. Over time the rash progresses and develops blisters that can be severe enough for categorization as third-degree burns. Many children with severe SJS are treated in hospital burn units.

SJS is extremely rare. In the United States, the incidence of SJS is estimated to be between 2.6 and 7.1 cases per one million persons per year. Most scientists believe SJS is caused by an allergic-type reaction to medications, although the exact cause is still being debated. Besides eye problems, SJS also causes a variety of skin lesions inside as well as outside the body. Symptoms from the SJS have left Jeanne with significant scaring on her intestines. As a result, she underwent an intestinal "triple bypass."

The bypass surgery triggered reactive airway disease (RAD). RAD is also frequently referred to as pediatric asthma. Symptoms include recurrent wheezing and coughing, fever, and altered mental states. Pediatric asthma, or RAD, is a leading cause of hospitalization, chronic disease, and school absenteeism. In severe cases of RAD, damage to the lungs can accumulate over time to such a degree that the airways become permanently narrowed.

Jeanne's life seems almost like a strong onion that is slowly being peeled back, layer by layer. At each step of the way, there is strong emotion and some physical reaction. At this point in the interview, I notice that Jeanne is smiling. She says she is smiling because her list of maladies seems almost comical to her when she thinks about her whole life as a young person. She continues to add to the list.

"Then later I got epilepsy. And that's about it," she states matter-of-factly with a smile. Jeanne continues to battle epileptic seizures and breathing problems on a routine basis. She sleeps with oxygen at night, which makes her feel "a little bit different."

"At first, when I began to understand all this, I was just a little upset. I felt really like different from everyone else, but now I am beginning to accept that it's in the past. And even though it has affected me now, I am just going to have to accept it and try to be a normal person."

While she works hard to accept her illness, she believes others run away from it, and thus from her.

"I think people keep their distance, because my mom is like that. She is afraid to tell me stuff sometimes, because she is afraid of saying the wrong things, or she knows she can't do anything about it, except take me to the doctors and try to get medicine. My dad has relied more on faith. He'll just pray to God, and I tell him that I don't really have that faith right now. And he says to keep doing it. I really don't like to communicate with my father about that," she adds.

Jeanne was only four when she encountered leukemia. She vaguely remembers some of her many days spent in the hospital, including the health care professionals, especially the nurses, who went out of their way to be funny so that she would have more good than bad days. Despite their best intentions, physicians frightened Jeanne more so than the nurses.

"The nurses explained a lot to me. I guess I got to be better friends with the nurses, since they were there longer than the doctors." She also says that the physicians seemed to know before anyone else that something bad was going to happen.

"Doctors? I know I didn't really like them coming, so I kind of got under my covers and stuff when they came. I was kind of scared," she recalls.

Remission is a good word for cancer patients like Jeanne. Yet there are many more bad words. For Jeanne, the bad-word dictionary includes words and phrases like surgery, has come back, seizures, found something there, and new medication. Jeanne does not specifically remember being told she was sick.

"I do remember some stuff in the hospital. But I don't really remember pain or anything. I know my mother told me that I told her, 'Mommy, I know I'm sick.' "

As with many ill children and young people, there is much conversation with Jeanne about sibling interaction and support. In Jeanne's case, she is very close to her sister and her brother from whom she received her bone marrow, yet their relationships are not without sibling consternations. One of the benefits Jeanne derives from talking with her mature younger sister is that her sister will keep things to herself.

"I feel weird when more people know about my illness. I guess I'm kind of in the center of stuff, and I don't like to be because I'm very shy."

Yet things are not always good between the sisters. "My sister feels like she's being deprived of attention. She tells me sometimes, and I can see how she feels, too, and I feel bad. I'm not trying to be at the center of attention, but I'm usually the one people ask about," she adds.

Jeanne is also embarrassed when her younger sister has to take care of her, like when they go out together.

"I just feel like, weird. If me and my sister go out, and I'm having seizures, they want my sister to watch over me, and I feel really different because I'm the older one that is supposed to be watching over her."

She is grateful for her brother's bone marrow that has kept her in remission for many years. Nonetheless, the issue is not without tension.

"He's going to college and stuff, and even though we fight a lot, a couple of times he has brought up the bone marrow he gave me. 'Well, I gave you your bone marrow' type thing. I don't know, it's just kind of sad because he can bring that against me and stuff. And my parents have, too. Like if I get mad at my brother, they will tell me, 'He gave you your bone marrow,' so . . . I don't know, it's just really weird."

At times Jeanne believes talking about her illness "makes it worse" because "soon everyone will know." Nonetheless, one of the persons with whom she must talk about her illness is her primary pulmonary specialist.

Jeanne thinks her physician is a "good doctor. She's kind of straightforward," she adds. Yet at times, hearing straightforward talk is hard.

"She said if I had gotten pneumonia, if I can get a lung transplant, then I would be alright, maybe. And if I didn't get a new lung, then I was just going to die. I don't know, sometimes it just kind of hurts."

"I come out of the office crying a lot. I think about death and stuff—that I will be gone." Jeanne suggests a better approach on the part of physicians and others might seem to be a "little more informative, and don't like, say it straightforward. Just tell them what can happen if you do or don't . . . just use a little bit more sensitive words than die or pass on."

La malita means "the sick one." That term and its connotation is why Jeanne does not like talking about her illness with her family. Yet that is how she is consistently identified.

"It feels weird, kind of, being known like that. That's a little embarrassing. That's a bad thing when a lot of people know." Jeanne explains that her mother consistently has to remind family members that she is the mother of other children as well when they only ask about one child because she is ill.

One might think someone as beautiful and kindhearted as Jeanne would be as popular in high school as the homecoming queen. Yet she suggests such is not the case.

"I don't have a lot of friends just because I feel like I'm shy, and I feel a lot different than them, so I don't feel like I should be with them." When asked specifically how she feels different, she replies, "Just the way I am, the way my past was and stuff."

Jeanne is especially close, however, to two friends whom she has known a long time. "He (referring to one of her friends) just tells me how strong I am, and he would have given up, and stuff like that." Jeanne says talk like that makes her feel better because it makes her know, "I guess, that I'm doing the right thing."

Jeanne spends a lot of her time wondering if she is doing the right thing. She also spends a lot of her time telling her two friends and sister that she likes to take care of herself most of the time so that they will not continually remain behind with her as she struggles to physically keep up.

Beyond thinking about her physical issues, Jeanne is no longer interested in spiritual talk, because "God is not listening," she says. "I'm Catholic. I used to be really into that, but lately I really don't have any faith anymore. I'm starting to give up on stuff like that, because I have prayed and prayed that 'I hope I get better soon.' Then it just seems like every year, something else goes wrong. I feel like He's not listening or something.

"I'm starting to really give up on faith now. And I guess my father is like, really religious, and he wants me to stay a Catholic and wants me to get back my faith, but I don't know, I guess he's not really helping me with getting back my faith. We go to mass, and to me it's kind of boring. I just want to go to a church that's outgoing, kind of, that will get you in the spirit. He doesn't want to do that. He said that we have to go to where he wants to go until we are 18 and out of the house. And I don't know, he doesn't let us explore new stuff like that. And I wish he would." This is an area of tension between Jeanne and her dad, and to a lesser extent, her mother.

"Mom's more easygoing about that, and she is willing to take us to some churches. But both of them want us to believe in God. I just want to explore different churches and different religions to see where I fit in."

Jeanne adds that soon she hopes to get a car for her 18th birthday or possibly that Christmas. Some of the first places she plans on driving to are new churches in the area.

In order to be perceived as just like everyone else, Jeanne sometimes withholds medical information from her parents. "Yeah, I have done that a lot of the times" (not told her parents she was feeling badly).

"Sometimes, I guess, when I tell them, it seems like they get mad at me, but they say they are mad at the illness. That's why they get upset. But I don't know. I know when I'm about to have a seizure, they want me to tell, but a lot of times I don't. I just go along with it."

Jeanne wonders at times about the hardships her illness has placed on those around her.

"I think that my parents' relationship would be better, because a lot of times I feel like I'm just a waste of money type thing. They have just spent a lot of money on me because of health stuff.

"Maybe if I had never gotten sick, they would still have that money and stuff. I don't know. I'm not sure. That's just something I think, because when we get bills, it's usually because of my doctors and stuff, and I just think that. Yeah, maybe my parents would have been better off, like had a better relationship at the place where they lived before they moved because of my illness."

Despite her shyness, Jeanne has a strong story to tell, and she wants to tell it. In meeting a new person who had cancer, she says she would first share with her or him her own personal experiences.

"First I would tell them about my story, and I guess, just tell them that I will be there if they ever need me to talk to, just to help out along the way. I know they have family, but sometimes a stranger or a friend can help better in some ways. I don't know, I would just be there for them and everything."

Stories are important in Jeanne's life because "I like to read. It just helps to know there are other people out there going through the same thing and stuff."

Some day Jeanne would like to write her own story in the form of a book. She mentioned she likes true stories, like *Jay's Journal* and *Go Ask Alice*. *Jay's Journal* is a story about a young boy's addiction to drugs and Satanism before his suicide at age 16. *Go Ask Alice* is a chronicle of information designed specifically for young people concerned with physical, sexual, and emotional health.

Jeanne battled depression when she was in the sixth grade. She continues to struggle with finding her own healthy way as a shy and somewhat alone individual. "That's what *Jay's Journal* is about (depression and searching). Jay believed in God at first, and he started exploring, and kind of went the wrong path, and stuff like that. I thought of Satanism, but after I read the book, I knew it wasn't a good idea," she says.

Regardless of any spiritual path she may or may not take, Jeanne's short-term goals are to get her driver's license and graduate with her class from high school. She hopes to be able to go to college. She also would like to volunteer her time with the Big Brothers, Big Sisters program once she turns 18. She definitely likes working with children and young people. Eventually she hopes to have her own family and children.

In the meantime, she will continue to think about her life and the choices she needs to make in terms of which roads to travel.

Right now, Jeanne is not only concerned about shopping at the bookstore next door for a Christmas present for her sister, she is also worried about bigger issues, like whether or not to undergo a lung transplant. In her spare time from schoolwork, she does research on the pros and cons of lung transplantation given her particular types of medical problems. Her physicians want Jeanne to move forward with the transplant.

"Yeah, they are wanting to do a transplant, so I'll research that. And they are thinking of also doing another brain surgery for my epilepsy. I still have to get tested for that. I do research for that, because they say if they do it, there is a chance that I will have weakness in my left arm, or that I might be paralyzed, so I'm trying to do a lot of research."

Life's handouts have put more on the plate of this painfully shy and gorgeous Jackie Kennedy Onassis look-alike in 17 brief years than most senior citizens experience in entire lifetimes. As our interview drew to a close and the java man announced the readiness of a grande cappuccino decaf, I was acutely aware then, and remain so now, of the remarkable attitude of this beautiful 17-year-old young woman, inside and out. Her future stakes and decisions are considerable.

After the first of the 2004 New Year, I contacted Jeanne via e-mail to see if she had made any decision on whether to seek a transplant. I also wanted to see in general how she was doing. She responded:

"I'm doing alright. My breathing had gotten bad last week, but it's doing better. How are you? I didn't get a car for Christmas and was kinda sad but I did get a picture phone, so that was okay. For my birthday ..., I had a BBQ with family and friends. Then ..., I had a little get-together with some of my friends, and finally ..., I went to my first club .... Hehe. It was fun and that was the end of my B-Day celebration.... How was your Christmas and New Year's Eve? I still haven't made the decision on whether or not I want a lung transplant, but I'm leaning more towards yes. Well, thanks for the email."

Epilogue

In 2008 Jeanne continues to do well in managing her illness, and in the midst of doing so she is moving forward. Since meeting me at the coffee shop right before that Christmas, Jeanne has married and is studying to be a medical assistant. Graduation is expected in a few short months. In the spirit of life being full of connections, Jeanne will complete part of her graduation requirements by working in the office of the oncologist who initially diagnosed her at the age of four.

Jeanne has not yet had a lung transplant, although in her last evaluation her lungs were shown to be a little worse than before. She continues to ponder the possibility of another brain surgery in order to reduce or eliminate seizures. She is the proud mother of a healthy baby boy.

Quiet Considerations
An Interviewer's Perspective

A Lesson Learned – *Soloing*

In flying lessons, everyone must solo. Perhaps this is true in life as well.

After talking with Jeanne at the bookstore, I was struck by how much of her life she seemed to be managing by *soloing*, except for the close relationship she talked of with her sister. This is certainly not to cast judgments on her parents, for Jeanne may indeed have been very close to them. It's just that from the interview discussion, she seemed to be flying her plane mostly on her own – and be completely content to do so at age 17.

Perhaps there is a lesson here in recognizing that dealing with chronic or terminal illnesses means that part of the time we are flying solo. No one else is getting the chemotherapy treatments for us. No one else is directly experiencing our own medical tests or radiation treatments. At some level, we're all on our own.

Suggested Response Strategies/Discussion Questions/ Commentary:

** Find sources of personal inspiration and comfort for when times are extremely tough and setbacks occur. If possible, read books about people who have spent considerable amounts of time alone and/or in fearful situations.

** Inform those around you as to whether you are comfortable dying alone. Vigils that last for 24-hours-a-day, seven-days-a-week over long periods of time can be difficult to maintain for loved ones.

** Learn to be alone with your own thoughts. Do not feel obligated to share with others your innermost thoughts, unless you care to do so.

** Continue your journal writing process.

Your Personal Notes/Action Steps:

-13-

ENOUGH

When I walk into the small hospital room, 18-year-old Ryan is talking to his young-looking mother. His mother says to me with a smile: "I'm going to leave you two alone. He'll talk more if I'm not around." With that, she leaves the room.

Turning to Ryan, a striking, congenial-looking, fair-haired young man, I say hello. He is propped up on pillows, dressed in street clothes, lying under a white hospital blanket. A worn baseball cap covers his head.

Although he does not smile often during the interview, when we first meet, his long, angular face breaks into a tight smile. Ryan has a quiet and strong countenance about him.

Nothing about Ryan's physical well-being appears out of the ordinary except that he is lying in a hospital bed in street clothes. He tells me he is hoping to go home that day. A laptop computer is positioned on top of the blanket. He has been surfing the Internet.

Ryan and I chat briefly about what he was doing on his computer, and I thank him for agreeing to the interview. He shrugs and says, "No problem." On the surface, one would think Ryan has not a care in the world beyond that of any normal teenage male.

As I sit down and look around the room for a plug for the tape recorder, I notice an interesting item lying on top of a small hospital table to the right of his bed. During prior interviews with other patients, I had observed a host of medical equipment like intravenous fluid bags, hangers, oxygen units, beepers and so on, almost to the point that such items had become routine to me over time. But today this particular item was something I had never seen before in any of my interviews and had never really thought about until that precise moment: an artificial leg.

Certainly I have seen quite a few people walking with artificial legs, but I have never looked at one disconnected from its master. This particular leg is positioned sideways on the table, almost like an old bathrobe lying on a bed. Nothing is around it. It is just there in plain view.

The leg seems somewhat strange to me at first in that the shiny, long metal rod that screamed *high tech* slid down into an old, worn tennis shoe at the end. This contrast of the old and the new, the shiny metal next to the ragged canvas, seems peculiarly sweet yet melancholy to me, for want of a better description.

Ryan notices that I had seen the leg. He asks, "Ever seen a $40,000 leg?"

"Can't say that I have," is my reply. He tells me the leg is his. I ask him if the leg has a name, and he says no.

Having become increasingly sensitive to the high emotional and economic costs of being sick, I ask Ryan if his family had to pay for the leg out of their own pockets, since he was the one who mentioned the price tag. He quickly replies no, thanks to the extensive efforts of his physician in lobbying the insurance company. His parents tell me the same thing later on when I talk with them in the hospital waiting room outside Ryan's room. The expressions of relief on their faces were universal and huge.

Ryan watches me set up my tape recorder. He says nothing. I think about this 18-year-old young man who is wearing a worn baseball cap and who now has one long angular leg and a stump and a metal rod for his other leg. He begins by telling me about his life and how he came to have an artificial leg.

Sandy-haired Ryan is an athlete who loves sports. He has played baseball, lifted weights, and participated in other athletic adventures. In fact, his initial wake-up call to physical problems came when he was playing baseball.

"I sprained my ankle playing baseball, and then I had x-rays for that. Then a month after that I started getting pains a little bit below my knee. Then I had an x-ray for that, and it showed up as a tumor," he states in a direct, matter-of-fact way. The word *tumor* immediately signaled to Ryan and his parents that he had cancer, even though at first the doctor never indicated whether the tumor was benign or malignant.

"It was just a regular doctor's office, and they said they saw the x-ray, and they said it was a tumor. So we pretty much . . . you could make that assumption that a tumor is cancerous," he adds. "We went to the one bone specialist, and they weren't sure, so they had to go all the way in there and test it and make sure and every-thing. So yeah, it was cancerous."

Ryan comments that his one bone doctor just said, "Oh you got this, there."

"Yeah, basically he tells it how it is, I guess. That's one way to do it. He doesn't feel sympathy for anybody," Ryan says. Ryan went on to say that his physician "just has to do his job . . . to help you."

Eighteen-year-old Ryan suffers from osteogenic sarcoma, also known as osteosarcoma, which is how Ryan and his family identify the disease. Although the disease itself is relatively rare, osteosarcoma is the most frequent form of bone cancer, found most commonly in young people ages 15 to 25. More than 90 percent of the tumors are formed in the growing ends of the bones. More than 80 percent of the osteosarcomas sites are found around the knees. Osteosarcoma accounts for approximately five percent of all childhood cancers. Most cases are caused by non-inheritable DNA errors in the bone. Osteosarcoma can spread throughout the body.

"It's called osteosarcoma. It's a bone cancer. It was found in 2001 in my tibia in my leg. They took out half my tibia, and then I had chemo for six months after that. And then about six months after finishing chemo, it reoccurred in my lungs. I had three lesions. Two of them were cancerous. They removed those. Another six months of chemo. And then six months after that, it showed up in my tibia again. So this time it was amputation," he adds.

"I haven't had any chemo yet or anything like that this time around. They can't give me any more. So they are going to have to find some other treatment to give me that will hopefully kill it."

Ryan continues to talk about the progression of his disease. "They have already found a few more lesions on my lungs. They are not sure what they are yet. They are pretty sure they might be cancer. But they are not sure yet."

I ask when he will know for sure. He explains, "Not until I have a biopsy or until they see them start growing. I have already had three chest x-rays, three chest cat-scans (CTs), and they have all stayed the same size. They haven't grown yet, so they will have the possibility of them not being there."

What is life like for an 18-year-old person who has already lost a leg to bone cancer and may be facing lung cancer for a second time without the option of receiving additional chemotherapy?

"I don't know. You can't do anything about it any-way, so you just make do. I just let them do what they have to do. That's it," Ryan states. He tells me that his parents worry more about his illness than he does.

Ryan answers many of my questions with short, terse answers. My sense is that while he voluntarily consented to an interview at the request of his physi-cian, he gets easily frustrated when the answers are not completely clear. In fact, he expresses that frustration with me. When I ask him in what ways he thinks other people might describe him, he replies: "I've been asked that before, and I still don't know. I don't like questions like that because they make me think—I don't like questions where it's not exact. It's not like math where the answer is this or this. I hate that. It's got to be one answer."

When I ask Ryan why he consented to an interview, he shrugs and replies, "I didn't have anything better to do, how about that?"

On this particular day he is back in the hospital because of an ailment similar to a collapsed lung. It is the second time he has had this problem in the past two months.

"I don't know what causes it. It happens to a lot of people that are my build, tall and skinny. I had it before last month. It could be from like a jolt, like getting hit in the side or something. Numerous things can cause it," he explains.

When this happened the last time, Ryan had a chest tube inserted to alleviate the problem. This time they are simply monitoring him to make sure it does not get worse.

"You can feel it. It hurts when you breathe in. Like yesterday, I started breathing in, and it just started hurting. And I felt it, and I knew it felt like from before."

When I ask him if he becomes aggravated over having the same medical problems once again that have occurred before so recently, he replies, "Nah. You can't stop it. There is nothing you can do about it."

The other piece of Ryan's medical equation will be unfolding soon when the test results show whether or not the new lung lesions are cancerous. He seems unfazed to the point of being nonchalant about the possibility of having cancer again.

"Yes—have/had. Oh I guess I still have it," he says.

The only time Ryan remembers being truly upset about having cancer was upon his initial diagnosis. His parents later reaffirmed how hard receiving the news was for everyone.

"I got an upset stomach, like that, but I couldn't do anything about it anyway. You just have to deal with it," he states. Later his father told me that Ryan vomited upon hearing the news. His father had wept openly.

"Maybe sometimes I worry, but it's nothing big. I guess most of the time when I worry, it's about when I have to get the scans to find out if it actually is it again. It's good to know, but if it is cancer again, I'm pretty bummed. But you can't do anything about it anyway," he repeats.

While Ryan and his parents and brother wait on the latest test results, Ryan takes things a step at a time. "I just go on." He does not think about the future in a long-term way, but rather he says he goes "day by day."

As the interview moves on, I become acutely aware of the magnitude of Ryan's willingness to talk with me in the first place. He is not a young man who cares to talk at all, including about his illness.

"I mean you've already heard the worst that's already going to happen, so why bring it up again? I mean, it's not going to help or anything. I mean it might help some people, but not me," he adds with a shrug. He does not talk about his illness with his friends. "We're not really that close. We just hang out and do stuff. They wouldn't care if I . . . ," he says as his voice trails off without completing the sentence.

Of all the adversities that have come his way, I ask Ryan which has been the worst thus far.

"I guess all three times were the worst. The leg physician just tells it like it is. He just comes in there and tells you what you have, and what they are going to do, and that's it. Like this time, he showed me, 'Yeah, you have a tumor, and we are going to amputate,' and that's it," Ryan recalls. That is when Ryan became pretty bummed, and his stomach turned sour.

Ryan says sometimes he jokes about his illness, depending on those around him. He does not joke with his parents because they worry a lot. At one point in the interview, he states that he worries more than his parents. Then he immediately corrects himself and says they worry more than he does. I did not press him on the issue. "You just have to deal with it," he says again.

"I make jokes about having a stump now because it's funnier to joke about it than to whine about it."

Before Ryan's leg was amputated, he was in his freshmen year in college studying computer science. Because he was surfing the Internet before I arrived, I ask Ryan if he uses the web to gather research about his illness or talk with other young people with the same disease, as other cancer patients had expressed to me was important in their own situations.

"I don't ever talk to anybody in here or anything. My parents go to the little web sites where you can talk to other people who have it—the same illness as you. Why? I mean, they have it. Woo hoo. They have it. I have it, too. That's how I see it, I don't know."

For the time being, Ryan will continue to await more information on the new lesions on his lungs. He has not been going to school because "I can't really walk around the hills out there. Plus, I'm having the physical therapy to learn how to walk good before I go back. So that's basically it. I'll go home, and everyone else will go to school or work, and I'll stay home and watch TV, surf the net, play video games."

One of the strongest components of Ryan's constitution that he conveys throughout the interview is his intense desire to be self-sufficient. At one point in our conversation, I notice his lips quivering slightly. I ask if he ever cries about having cancer. He replies succinctly, "No."

When I probe further simply by repeating the word *no* in an interrogatory fashion, he adds, "I don't think there's a reason to—nothing to cry about." He also comments that he does not think there is anything he has done in his life that "I'm proud of."

As we close the interview, I ask Ryan about his brother in terms of something that Ryan might find to be proud of in his life so far. Specifically I ask him if he would take care of his brother if anything happens to him. Ryan replies, "He's self-sufficient, too."

Perhaps in my own desire to end each interview on a more positive than negative note, especially this particular interview since it is my last in the series, I ask Ryan what he would want people to think or say about him right now at age 18, a young man with an expensive artificial leg. He thought for a long time and then replies, "That he's okay to be around, I guess."

As I walk out of Ryan's room and head for the elevator to leave the hospital, Ryan's mother is sitting in the colorful child-like waiting area with a gentleman two chairs over. I had seen the gentleman a few times before that day walking the halls. He seemed worried and sad as he walked and paced, his shoulders slumped and his face burrowed. Ryan's mother motions for me to come over and join them.

A Parents' Perspective

Ryan's mom, Dee, introduces me to her husband and Ryan's father, Ralf. Together they seem verbally and visually anxious for feedback on the interview with their son. Their primary interest is bottom-line basic, for they immediately ask me almost in unison, "Did he talk?"

For the next hour, I have the privilege of sitting with Dee and Ralf as they share with me their own perspectives in dealing with their oldest son's illness. I have not planned nor specifically requested the opportunity to interview them given Ryan's adult status of 18. However, parental perspectives are extremely important in understanding this unique time in young peoples' lives. Thus I ask if I can record our conversation. They willingly agreed. They are hungry to talk, almost to the opposite extreme as their son was tight lipped.

Dee and Ralf seem incredibly young to have a son Ryan's age. They explain to me that they married very young. They have been married for over twenty years.

Throughout most of the interview, Dee and Ralf cry. Unlike most of the former interviews, I must admit that I cry with them. I have been able to keep myself from tearing up in all but a handful of the previous interviews. I cry with them at times because they are hurting so badly, watching their firstborn experience cancer for possibly the third time with treatment doors closing all around them.

I also cry because they individually and collectively seem like such genuinely nice people. Self-described as opposites, Dee tells me she works in education, and Ralf works outdoors, thus his weathered skin and blue jeans. He strikes me as a rough and tough cowboy type who prefers not to have people see him cry, but those days are long gone. Today he is sitting in front of a total stranger crying like a weary baby.

One of the most interesting perspectives in talking with Ryan's parents is that, without betraying confidences, they are able to help fill in some of the missing blanks in my interview with their son. After talking with them, I am reminded that stories are simply snap-shots of what people say or do at that time, without the benefit of the screen before or after.

Ralf and Dee tell me that when Ryan was first diagnosed, he used the Internet to meet others who had cancer, including a young female friend whom he went to visit, thanks to the financial goodwill of family friends. They also explain to me that Ryan has always been an aficionado of computer games, and that somehow his stranger friends on the Internet became aware of his illness. As such, they posted a notice to all those who liked to play similar games. He then received over 600 "best wishes" e-mails from total strangers across the world, including Japan, Australia, Switzerland, and others. Ryan, "Mister I'd Rather Not Talk About It," took the time to personally answer most of them. Ryan never mentioned any of this in our conversation.

Dee expresses some level of frustration at Ryan's willingness to talk with cyberspace strangers about his illness, but not to his parents or his brother. Nonetheless, she seems grateful that he is talking at all.

"I think he keeps everything—not that he keeps everything in—he just takes everything in stride," Dee comments.

Having said that, Ralf and Dee both marvel at their son's strength: emotional and physical. They recall a time when the family went to Disneyland for Ryan's Make-a-Wish trip right after Ryan had been playing paintball with one of his cancer nurses. During the paintball game, Ryan fractured his leg before it had to be amputated. He said nothing about hurting his leg until walking around the theme park when his knee began swelling.

"His knee started swelling up a little bit, and he was saying that it was hurting him. And we were like, oh my gosh, we were all scared to death," Dee says. "And come to find out, he had fractured it playing paintball, and by the time that he got in (to see the physician), it had healed over. And they said that was good though because the calcification made it stronger. Yet it (the cancer) came back there, unfortunately."

From talking with Ryan's parents, a perspective becomes clear as to why their son might be terse at times in his own communication. Despite talking a great deal and crying even more, Ryan's dad does not mince words.

"Basically, it sucks because what choice do you have?" Ralf says through his tears, specifically commenting on the amputation. "That's the way Ryan deals with it. He's always joked about stuff. And as far as talking—"

"He's never talked about it," Dee finishes the sentence for her husband.

"I always wondered if Ryan knew what was going on," Ralf says. "I asked him one time. And I got the answer, 'Yes, I'm not stupid.' "

"I said, 'That's fine.' I smiled and let it go. You know, I'm not—it's just hard," he adds as he wipes his eyes.

Communication experts point to the importance of nonverbal and verbal cues in understanding communication interactions. Both Ryan's parents say wonderful things about the medical personnel. In fact, the staff has become extended members of the family. Reading their faces has become an important and telling ritual.

"You can see in their faces that it hurts them to deliver bad news to Ryan and the family repeatedly," Dee comments. Dee tells me that yes, the staff sometimes cry when they know Ryan's cancer has returned.

Ralf tells me no, they do not cry. Together they explain.

"No, not in front of Ryan. With us," Dee clarifies.

"They know. They know. You can see them, you know, the doctor, it hurts," Ralf says.

"It's scary," Dee adds.

Ralf and Dee also say that they themselves try not to cry too much in front of Ryan.

"We try to be strong for him, that's true," Dee says.

"We try not to cry. We try to hide it," Ralf adds.

Both parents add that despite their intentions, Ryan has seen them cry repeatedly in the last three years of their medical journey.

"He knows we are worried about it," Ralf says. Both parents also tell me their younger son is concerned about the situation as well.

"You know that he's getting the raw end of—anything," Dee says.

"You know, he's seen that we favor him (Ryan) a little bit more. You know, he's seen us. I've talked to him. He knows," Ralf adds.

Ralf and Dee have similar yet different perspectives on Ryan's thinking at this point in the disease process. Dee states she believes her firstborn is stubborn, and that out of the stubbornness and strength come his ability to always take things in stride, including cancer. Both parents believe some of their son's strong and terse constitution is nothing more than the typical defiance of any 18 year old, ill or not.

One of the most important components for Ryan in terms of his illness, according to his parents, relates to his wanting to be just like everyone else. He hates being looked upon as different.

"You know the one thing, too, the chemo stuff, when he lost his hair, the principal, I went to see her,"

Dee says. "She said Ryan can wear his cap to school. All he has to do is carry a little note. I told him and he said, 'No, it won't bother me.' He still says, 'I'm not handicapped.' You know, he hates to use the handicapped parking sign. He did use it when he was going to college. It was hard. That was before they removed the leg. It was hurting real bad to walk and stuff. And you know, we would be in the car together. We will use the sign so he doesn't have to walk so far, because he's getting used to the leg. He doesn't like it. He says, 'We don't need to park here. Park down there. I'm not handicapped.' "

"And then you get tired of asking, 'are you okay?' He gets frustrated with us, every five minutes us asking him that—sometimes, yeah, sometimes he gets angry. He's been like that since he was itty bitty," Ralf says.

Once again I find myself amazed at the determination, vulnerability, and honesty of those two kind individuals. Their willingness to share their story and gut-wrenching hurt with a total stranger is amazing. As I close the interview, I ask both Dee and Ralf about their future. They are hopeful now that Ryan is aging into adulthood, he will become eligible for new medical clinical trials and thus receive different kinds of treatment that could stop his cancer from occurring again.

In the meantime, they talk at length about their mutual desire not to see their 18-year-old son hurt anymore. They are worried about the future, and they cry openly. Their son amazes them in terms of his resolve and strength, for whatever the reasons. They intend to hold tight to one another and Ryan and his brother, each in their own respective ways.

"There's no reason for this to break a family," Ryan's father says steadfastly.

Talking helps sometimes, especially for Ryan's mother. Crying is inevitable for both of them.

"Don't put off anything you plan to do. Don't take anything for granted," Ralf tells me. "When I'm around Ryan, I'm better." Dee echoes the same sentiment.

"It's hard. I just can't believe that we are going through all of this," Dee says. "Once—okay. Twice—maybe. Three times, boy, it's like, okay, that's enough. You know, so we just think that we aren't going to get through it."

The youthful-looking mother continues with her sorrowful lamentation as if she were saying her prayer out loud to anyone who would listen. "You know, just let him go on with his life. Let him live his life. He's only 18. He's just starting out college, you know, trying. He's doing great with that leg. That's not bothering him."

Ralf was unable to speak any longer. Dee looks over at him and says to me: "I pray all the time. I say to keep him cancer free, give it to me. You know, he (Ryan) has never disliked it. And that's one thing that he has never said: 'It's not fair, why me?' Not one time. I've said it enough for—" Dee cannot finish the sentence because of her tears. I finish for her, "—all of you." She and Ryan's dad both look down and uniformly nod yes. They had had enough.

Epilogue

According to his physician, Ryan died peacefully at home several months after we talked.

Enough
An Interviewer's Perspective

A Lesson Learned – *Ending*

In the course of conducting these various interviews, I was consistently asked by friends and family how I was undertaking such a perceived sad, hard, and lonely task. Most of the time I would reply that things were going fine and that meeting such wonderful people was inspirational, a true statement without exception.

Yet after meeting Ryan and his parents, I knew I could take no more, for I was extremely emotional after these particular interviews. What I think happened is that all of the emotions and thoughts and senses of the entire set of interviews came to a head after talking with wonderful Ryan and his mom and dad. It was time for *ending* the interview series.

Endings of any kind are usually difficult. Yet the finality of death is without exception the most painful to experience and understand. For many of the young, brave, determined, and willing people I interviewed, their endings came far too soon at young ages. Yet their memories and those of all the survivors remain forever etched in my heart and mind. For all of those connected with this book, I say a heartfelt thank you.

Suggested Response Strategies/Discussion Questions/ Commentary:

** In a perfect world, what do you want your own personal ending to look like? How are you going to make that happen?

** Read these stories with others in a group, and talk together about what they have said to you about life in general and in particular, about your own life.

** What does life's ending mean for you in terms of living in the moment, here and now?

Your Personal Notes/Action Steps:

Life changes fast.
Life changes in the instant.
You sit down to dinner and life as you know it ends.
Joan Didion, Author

THEIR STORIES, OUR LESSONS

Within the hearts and minds of these unique story-tellers, like Minister David, Unfiltered Harry, and all the rest, come many wonderful hand-holding hints for use during end-of-life times. The stories are ours to individually read and ponder and analyze as we wish. Hopefully the lessons learned around the perspectives of *knowing, dreaming, studying, celebrating, persevering, listening, telling the truth, giving voice, balancing, disbanding, accepting, soloing,* and *ending* are helpful.

Yet collectively they can help us know what to say, what not to say, how to reach out, and most importantly, how not to become distant, despondent, or immobilized when someone we know and love is dying.

The stories tell us there are specific strategies to communicate with persons known to be dying. Over and over again, the dying young people said this: Regardless of the difficulty of the situation, *Show Up* and *Stay Connected.*

Yet once we get there, what do we say? How do we say it? Again, the young people give us answers.

* **Listen:** Sometimes words are simply not needed. Silence can be golden and a touch magical. We need not talk endlessly about mundane topics because we are uncomfortable. Instead we should listen to the person who is ill, and take our cues from him/her.

When we talk, we should avoid telling our own story, and instead place our loved ones and their needs at the heart of the matter.

* **Avoid Sense-making Explanations:** Story reasons or endings are not ours to make. Avoid filling in the gaps by trying to explain why the illness or death situation is happening. Instead, just be genuinely present, compassionate, caring, and concerned. Now is a good time to be a friend and not a know-it-all philosopher.

* **Mirror the Talk:** Everyone thinks about and approaches death in unique ways. Most of the young people whom I interviewed by far preferred straight talk and the use of words like ill and relapse. For others, this may not be the case. Whatever seems to be the preference of the person who is ill, try to mirror that talk within reason and appropriateness. Avoid feeling the need to be constantly—and possibly insincerely—upbeat when the situation may be quite the opposite.

* **Ask Questions:** Now is a great time to be inquisitive and probing, within reason, to ascertain the feelings and needs of the ill or dying person. Questions like, *How can I help? Is there something specific you need? Can I help your family for you? Are you concerned about anything in particular?* These are great and important questions to help make a tough situation better.

* **Understand that Words Matter:** Words and phrases can hurt or heal. Certainly the way in which communication is delivered matters. Yet even before the delivery, the choice of words and phrases is important.

On the following pages are a few specific suggestions for talking with people who are dying or dealing
with chronic serious illnesses.

Language phrases found to be *offensive* when said by healthy individuals	*Preferred* language phrases/ behavioral strategies
"Everything happens for a reason."	"I am very sorry this is happening." -or- "You can always talk with me." -or- "I'm always here whenever you need someone." *Note:* If you say this, mean it, and be there for the person. Follow whatever words you say with action, e.g., by staying close to the individual who is ill; otherwise do not say it.
"You are going to be all right."	"I am here for you. Let me know how I can help you."
"This is God's will."	"I'm sorry this happened." (Say nothing about *why* this happened.)
"Keep praying hard."	"Is there anything I can do for you?"

Language phrases found to be *offensive* when said by healthy individuals	*Preferred* language phrases/ behavioral strategies
"Heaven is the perfect place."	"What I know for certain is that I am here for you now, and I will stay with you during this rough time." (Say nothing about where the ill person may or may not be going unless that person instigates the conversation. Instead just listen. Stay focused on the present, not the future.)
"One must not question things at this time."	"If I were in your shoes, I would have many questions, too. I just wish I had all the answers for you. What I know for certain is that I am here to listen."
"I know how you feel. When I was sick. . . ."	"I can only imagine how hard this must be, or how you must feel right now. Just know that I am here to help you, and I will stay and listen or just be here for you if you do not want to talk right now."

Language phrases found to be *offensive* when said by healthy individuals	Preferred language phrases/ behavioral strategies
	(Avoid comparisons with your own personal past experiences unless asked. The telling of such experiences can move the conversation away from the ill person, and/or more towards a competitive, *you think you've got it bad*, scenario).
"Don't worry."	"If you are worried right now or concerned about things, I think that is absolutely understandable. Just know that you don't have to worry alone. I will be here for you."
"Don't dwell on things. Be happy. Let's talk about some-thing else."	"Whatever you want to talk about or do today is exactly what I want to do as well."
"The books I've read say we should be. . . ." (e.g., focusing on the positive right now)	"To be perfectly honest, sometimes I'm not sure what to say, so please tell me if I say the wrong thing because I simply want to be helpful to you."

Language phrases found to be *offensive* when said by healthy individuals	*Preferred* language phrases/ behavioral strategies
"Are you OK? How's it going?"	"If you want to, tell me what kind of a day you are having today. I would like to know."
"Does it hurt?"	"Are you feeling uncomfort- able" -or- "Is there something I can get you?"
Notes	**Notes**

*..Two roads diverged in the wood, and I - -
I took the one less traveled by,
And that has made all the difference.*
Robert Frost, Poet

GOING FORTH

From the mouths of babes....

These young people, their families and medical team members talked straight from the heart during exceedingly difficult times. If they can do that, surely we can show up and be present to help others like them in our own lives.

Transitions are oftentimes difficult and unsettling. As our loved ones go through end-of-life experiences, or we go through them ourselves, knowing what to do and say and how to react is important. Hopefully this collection of narratives has provided readers with a glimpse into the lives of seriously ill and dying young people. Better yet, perhaps the conversations will give us all specific strategies and ideas for being present, being helpful, and staying connected.

Noted scholar W. G. Bartholome reminds us that:

Respect for dying children involves a series of challenges for their parents and their healthcare providers. It means a willingness to acknowledge our limited capacity to rescue them or protect them from death. . . . It means a willingness to respond to their experiences and to be truthful and to assist them in developing their own understanding of the reality they face. It demands that we respect their capacity for autonomy by allowing them to participate actively in making decisions about appropriate care.

And it means supporting them and their coping strategies as they attempt to maintain control over their lives to the end. It means, above all, a willingness and ability to trust that they can manage their own dying at least as well as big people.[4]

(Quoted with permission)

Whether we are big or little people, we will all die. It is a unique, spiritual, challenging, and chaotic time for many. May we all go forth and face this time in a spirit of openness, wonderment, connection and hand-holding. Let us be present and willing to learn from and engage in meaningful conversations with the youngest to the oldest. When we trip over ourselves, let us say we're sorry and try again. Let us learn about dying—*and living*—from the stories of others as we continue creating our own.

REFERENCES AND RESOURCES

Babbie, E. (2001). *The Practice of Social Research* (9th Ed.) Belmont, CA: Wadsworth/Thompson Learning.

Bartholome, W. G. (1993). Care of the dying child: The demand of ethics. *Second Opinion,* 18, 25-39.

Bateson, G. (1972). *Steps to an Ecology of Mind.* New York, NY: Ballantine.

Beck, C. S. (2001). *Communicating for Better Health: A Guide Through the Medical Mazes.* Needham Heights, MA: Allyn & Bacon.

Bluebond-Langner, M. (1977). Meanings of death to children. In H. Feifel (Ed.), *New Meanings of Death,* (pp. 47-66). New York, NY: McGraw-Hill.

Bluebond-Langner, M. (1978). *The Private Worlds of Dying Children.* Princeton, NJ: Princeton University Press.

Bluebond-Langer, M. (2002). *Decision making for children with cancer when cure is not likely: Scope of the problem and recommendations for clinical practice.* Rutgers University, Camden. Retrieved online at http://children.camden.rutgers.edu/BluebondStudy.htm.

Bochner, A. P., & Ellis, C. (1996). Talking over ethnography. In C. Ellis and A. P. Bochner (Eds.), *Composing Ethnography* (pp. 13-45). Walnut Creek, CA: Altamira Press.

Bricher, G. (1999). Pediatric nurses, children, and the development of trust. *Journal of Clinical Nursing,* 8, 451-459.

Brinchmann, B. S., Forde, R., & Nortvedt, P. (2002). What matters to the parents? A qualitative study of parents' expectations with life-and-death decisions concerning their premature infants. *Nursing Ethics,* 9, 388-404.

Browning, L. D. (1992). Lists and stories as organizational communication. *Communication Theory,* 24, 281-302.

Bruner, J. (1990). *Acts of Meaning.* Cambridge, MA: Harvard University Press.

Burton, L. (1975). *The Family Life of Sick Children: A Study of Families Coping with Chronic Childhood Disease.* Boston, MA: Routledge & Kegan Paul Ltd.

De Vries, B. (Ed.) (1999). *End of Life Issues: Interdisciplinary and Multidimensional Perspectives.* New York, NY: Springer Publishing Company, Inc.

Denzin, N. K., & Lincoln, Y. S. (1994). Entering the Field of Qualitative Research. In N. K. Denzin & Y. S. Lincoln (Eds.), *Handbook of Qualitative Research* (pp. 1-17). Thousand Oaks, CA: Sage Publications, Inc.

Dervin, B. (1989). Audience as listener and learner, teacher and confidante: The sense-making approach. In R. E. Rice & C. K. Atkin (Eds.), *Public Communication Campaigns* (2nd Ed.), (pp. 67-86). Newbury Park, CA: Sage Publications, Inc.

Devers, E., & Robinson, K. M. (2002). The making of a grounded theory: After death communication. *Death Studies, 26,* 241-253.

Didion, J. (2005). *The Year of Magical Thinking.* New York, NY: Alfred A. Knopf.

Faulkner, K. W. (1993). Children's understanding of death. In A. Armstrong-Dailey & S. Z. Goltzer (Eds.), *Hospice Care for Children* (pp. 9-21). New York, NY: Oxford University Press.

Fine, G. A., & Sandstrom, K. L. (1998). Knowing children: Participant observation with minors. In *Qualitative Research Methods, 15.* Newbury Park, CA: Sage Publications, Inc.

Fletcher, P. N. (2002). Experiences in family bereavement. *Family Community Health, 25,* 57-70.

Fowler-Kerry, S. (1990). Utilizing cognitive strategies to relieve pain in young children. In D. Tyler & E. Krane (Eds.), *Advances in Pain Research and Therapy, 15: Pediatric Pain,* (pp. 366-371). New York, NY: Raven Press.

Geertz, C. (1973). Thick description: Toward an interpretive theory of culture. In Geertz, C. (Ed.), *The Interpretation of Cultures* (pp. 3-30). New York, NY: Basic Books, Inc.

Geist-Martin, P., Ray, E. B., & Sharf, B. F. (2003). *Communicating Health: Personal, Cultural, and Political Complexities.* Belmont, CA: Wadsworth.

Gilbert, K. R. (2002). Taking a narrative approach to grief research: Finding meaning in stories. *Death Studies, 26,* 223-239.

Glaser, B. G., & Strauss, A. L. (1967). *The Discovery of Grounded Theory.* Chicago, IL: Aldine.

Goodman, J. E., & McGrath, P. J. (1991). The epidemiology of pain in children and adolescents: A review. *Pain, 46,* 247-264.

Judd, D. (1989). *Give Sorrow Words: Working with a Dying Child.* London: Free Association Books.

Kalish, R. A. (1976). Death and dying in a social context. In R. H. Binstock & E. Shanas (Eds.), *Handbook of Aging and the Social Sciences* (pp. 483-507). New York, NY: Van Nostrand Reinhold.

Kane, J., Hellsten, M. B., & Coldsmith, A. (2004) (in press). *Human Suffering: The Need for Relationship-based Research in Pediatric End-of-life Care.*

Kaufman, S. R. (2000). The clash of meanings. Medical narrative and biographical story at life's end. *Generations, 23,* 77-84.

Keeley, M. P. & Yingling, J. M. (2007). *Final Conversations: Helping the Living and Dying Talk to Each Other.* Acton, MA: VanderWyk & Burnham.

Kirk, J. & Miller, M. L. (1986). Reliability and validity in qualitative research. In *Qualitative Research Methods, 1,* (pp. 9-85). Newbury Park, CA: Sage Publications, Inc.

Koocher, G. P. (1974). Talking with children about death. *American Journal of Orthopsychiatry, 44,* 404-411.

Levi-Strauss, C. (1966). *The Savage Mind* (2nd Ed.). Chicago, IL: University of Chicago Press.

Lindlof, T. R. (1995). Qualitative communication research methods. In J. G. Delia (Ed.), *Current Communication: An Advanced Text Series, 3,* (pp. xi-314). Thousand Oaks, CA: Sage Publications, Inc.

Markham Shaw, C. L. (1997). Personal narrative: Revealing and reflecting others. *Human Communication Research, 24,* 302-320.

Miller, V.D., & Knapp, M.L. (1986). The post-nutio dilemma: Approaches to communicating with the dying. In M. McLaughlin (Ed.), *Communication Yearbook IX*, (pp. 723-738). Beverly Hills, CA: Sage Publications, Inc.

Milo, E. (1997). Maternal responses to the life and death of a child with developmental disability: A story of hope. *Death Studies, 21*, 443-477.

Morris, V. (2001). *Talking About Death Won't Kill You.* New York, NY: Workman Publishing Company, Inc.

Nagy, M. (1948). The child's theories concerning death. *The Journal of Genetic Psychology, 73*, 3-27.

Parry, J. K. & Shen Ryan, A. (Eds.), (1995). *A Cross-Cultural Look at Death, Dying, and Religion.* Chicago, IL: Nelson-Hall Publishers.

Patton, M. Q. (1990). Qualitative analysis and interpretation. In M. Q. Patton (Ed.), *Qualitative Evaluation and Research Methods* (pp. 371-424). Newbury Park: Sage Publications, Inc.

Pauly, J. J. (1991). A beginner's guide to doing qualitative research of mass communication. *Journalism Monographs, 125*, 1-29.

Puchalski, C. M. (2002). Spirituality and end-of-life care: A time for listening and caring. *Journal of Palliative Medicine, 5*, 289-294.

Riessman, C. K. (1993). Narrative analysis. *Qualitative Research Methods, 30*, Newbury Park, CA: Sage Publications, Inc.

Rubin, H. J. & Rubin, I. S. (1995). Interviews as guided conversation, and assembling the parts. In H. J. Rubin and I. S. Rubin (Eds.), *Qualitative Interviewing: The Art of Hearing Data*, (pp. 122-167). Thousand Oaks, CA: Sage Publications, Inc.

Shaw, E. (2005). *What to do When a Loved One Dies: A Practical and Compassionate Guide to Dealing with Death on Life's Terms.* Carlsbad, CA: Writeriffic Publishing Group.

Silverman, P. R. (2000). *Never Too Young to Know: Death in Children's Lives.* New York, NY: Oxford University Press.

Spinetta, J. J. & Deasy-Spinetta, P. D. (1979). *Talking With Children with a Life-threatening Illness: A Handbook for Health Care Professionals.* Rockville, MD: Cystic Fibrosis Foundation.

Sprang, G., & McNeil, D.S. (1995). *The Many Faces of Bereavement: The Nature and Treatment of Natural, Traumatic, and Stigmatized Grief.* New York, NY: Brunner/Mazel, Publishers.

Stepanek, M. (2002). *Celebrate Through Heart Songs.* New York, NY: Hyperion Books.

Thompson, T. L. (1989). Communication and dying: The end of the life-span. In J. Nussbaum (Ed.), *Life-span Communication: Normative Processes,* (pp. 339-359). Mahwah, NJ: Erlbaum Associates.

Wright, K., & Flemons, D. (2002). Dying to know: Qualitative research with terminally ill persons and their families. *Death Studies, 26,* 255-271.

Yedidia, M. J., & McGregor, B. (2001). Confronting the prospect of dying: Reports of terminally ill patients: *Journal of Pain and Symptom Management, 22,* 807-819.

FOOTNOTES

[1] Quotes from a pediatric pulmonary specialist, Dr. Martha
     Morse of Texas, taken from a 2003 feature article in a Texas
     newspaper. Used with permission.

[2] At the suggestion of the Ede family, information from
     various Internet sites such as the Patrick Ede CaringBridge
     web site found at http://www.caringbridge.org/tx/
     patrickede, along with a review of a video-taped church
     celebration led by his parents to thank friends and sup-
     porters, is used to supplement the interview commentary.

[3] Hutchings, D. (1998). Communicating with metaphor: A
     dance with many veils. *The American Journal of Hospice &
     Palliative Care, 15*, 282-284.

[4] Bartholome, W. G. (1993). Care of the dying child. The
     demand of ethics. *Second Opinion, 18*, 24-41. Permission
     granted by Park Ridge Center for the Study of Health,
     Faith, and Ethics, Park Ridge, IL.

ABOUT THE AUTHOR

Melody Chatelle holds a Ph.D. in Communication Studies from The University of Texas at Austin, where her dissertation, upon which *Journeys of Heartache and Grace* is based, was nominated for Dissertation of the Year.

Dr. Chatelle is a well-known and highly regarded public speaker, coach, and trainer who owns and operates Chatelle and Associates, an Austin-based communication and advocacy consulting firm.

A native of Texas, Dr. Chatelle is available to conduct workshops and training sessions throughout the country on end-of-life communication as she does with other parts of her core business. Chatelle and Associates specializes in business development, public relations, crisis media management, and legislative consulting.

For more information or to schedule a presentation or workshop on end-of-life communication, contact Dr. Melody Chatelle as follows:

Chatelle and Associates
5804 Harrington Cove, Austin, Texas 78731
1/512-502-9545 (phone) • 1/512-502-1044 (fax)
E-mail: mchatell@onr.com
www.chatelleandassociates.com
or
LangMarc Publishing
Post Office Box 90488
Austin, Texas 78709-0488
1/800-864-1648 (book orders)
1/512-394-0989 (information) • 1/512-394-0829 (fax)
langmarc@booksails.com
www.langmarc.com

Partial proceeds from the sale of this book will be used for the benefit of individuals or organizations supporting children and young people with serious or life-threatening illnesses.

221

— To Order This Book —

Journeys of Heartache and Grace
by Melody Chatelle, Ph.D.

If unavailable at your favorite bookstore,
we will fill your order promptly
—Postal Orders —
Chatelle and Associates
5804 Harrington Cove, Austin, Texas 78731
1/512-502-9545 (phone)
1/512-502-1044 (fax) or online
E-mail: mchatell@onr.com
www.chatelleandassociates.com
or
LangMarc Publishing
P.O. Box 90488 • Austin, Texas 78709-0488
To order online at www.langmarc.com
or call 1-800-864-1648
E-mail: langmarc@booksails.com

Journeys of Heartache and Grace
(Paperback) U.S.A. $16.95 + $3 postage
Texas residents add 8.25% sales tax
Canada: $20.95 + postage

Send _____ copies to:

Name: _____

Address: _____

_____

Check Enclosed: _____ Phone: _____

Credit card: _____
     Expiration: _____

Breinigsville, PA USA
07 October 2009
225418BV00001B/3/P